The Victor's Cry

The Victor's Cry

Joy McHale

© 2006 by Joy McHale. All rights reserved.

Pleasant Word (a division of WinePress Publishing, PO Box 428, Enumclaw, WA 98022) functions only as book publisher. As such, the ultimate design, content, editorial accuracy, and views expressed or implied in this work are those of the author.

No part of this publication may be reproduced, stored in a retrieval system or transmitted in any way by any means—electronic, mechanical, photocopy, recording or otherwise—without the prior permission of the copyright holder, except as provided by USA copyright law.

Unless otherwise noted, all Scriptures are taken from the Holy Bible, New International Version, Copyright © 1973, 1978, 1984 by the International Bible Society. Used by permission of Zondervan Publishing House. The "NIV" and "New International Version" trademarks are registered in the United States Patent and Trademark Office by International Bible Society.

Scripture references marked KJV are taken from the King James Version of the Bible.

Scripture references marked NASB are taken from the New American Standard Bible, © 1960, 1963, 1968, 1971, 1972, 1973, 1975, 1977 by The Lockman Foundation. Used by permission.

ISBN 1-4141-0703-X
Library of Congress Catalog Card Number: 2006901167

Dedication

Dad, thank you for always being there and giving your support and your faithful, unconditional love.

Mom, thank you for showing me the importance of being a woman after God's heart.

To my husband and best friend, Gene, thank you for your passionate love and leading me into a closer walk with the Lord

To my pastor and friend, Jerry Walls, for your support in this project and your belief in me. Thank you for being a man of God that firmly yet gently preaches the gospel of Jesus Christ.

Contents

Introduction	ix
Foreword	xi

WEEK ONE: LIVING OUT GOD'S PROMISES

Day One: Abraham's Belief	13
Day Two: Sarah's Joy	16
Day Three: Abraham's Obedience	18
Day Four: Isaac's Trust	20
Day Five: Right Choices	22

WEEK TWO: EFFECTIVE OBEDIENCE

Day One: When God Calls	25
Day Two: Ocean Revival	27
Day Three: The First Kings Bed and Breakfast	30
Day Four: One's Heart Cry	33
Day Five: Total Surrender	35

WEEK THREE: ALL OF MY MIND

Day One: Understanding the Battle Plan	39
Day Two: The Battle of Doubt	42
Day Three: The War on Worry	44
Day Four: The Landmine of Insecurity	47
Day Five: The Destruction of Pride	50

WEEK FOUR: ALL OF MY HEART

Day One: Esther's Bold Heart	53
Day Two: Job's Confident Heart	55
Day Three: David's Tender Heart	60
Day Four: Lydia's Open Heart	64
Day Five: Paul's Peaceful Heart	66

WEEK FIVE: HEART REPAIR

Day One: The Deceitful Heart	71
Day Two: The Wayward Heart	72
Day Three: The Broken Heart	75
Day Four: The Resting Heart	79
Day Five: The Restored Heart	81

WEEK SIX: ALL OF MY SOUL

Day One: Just As I Am	87
Day Two: The Potter's House	90
Day Three: A New Creation	94
Day Four: His Delight	98
Day Five: Salt of the Earth	100

WEEK SEVEN: ALL OF MY STRENGTH

Day One: Choosing to Rejoice	103
Day Two: Choosing to Believe	106
Day Three: Choosing to Obey	110
Day Four: Choosing to Serve	114
Day Five: The Victor's Cry	117

Introduction

I am so excited about The *Victor's Cry*! My prayer is you will not only learn more about loving the Lord with all of your heart, all of your soul, all of your strength, and all of your mind, but that you will live it. It is one thing to know that God has promises for you. It is something altogether different to live out those promises. Living out the promises God has for your life will enable you to live a life of effective obedience. Giving the Lord God all of your mind, conquering your battles and experiencing victory in your life will destroy the strongholds Satan desperately wants to keep you in. Allowing all of your heart to be given to the One who created you will free you from your past, and you will be overwhelmed by the perfect love that restores your heart through grace, mercy, peace, and joy. With all of your soul, seeking the One who has made you a new creation, you will find He delights in you just as you are.

God has a plan and a purpose for your life. This plan is a life of victory, to be lived with all of your strength in truth, belief, obedience, and rejoicing. You belong to the King of kings, the great I Am, the Prince of Peace, the One who welcomes you into His presence with gladness. Go forth, prepare yourself, lift high your banner, sound the battle cry–the victor's cry–for you are victorious.

Foreword

When Joy asked me to write this overview, I was excited. I met her when she was at Liberty University. I was her professor and she was a godly young lady. I knew that she had a wonderful life ahead of her. She desired to learn all she could and be the godly woman God desired that she would be. And she is. She is a teacher and I pray that many will learn from her.

What a wonderful book she has written to teach us how to understand that we are not the only ones who have had trials in our lives. This book presents seven great weeks to look at people in God's Word and see how they handled problems in their lives. Their choices in going through problems gave them the Victor's Cry.

In the first week of her book we look at Abraham, Sarah, and Isaac. What a great story of how they handled the problems and came through with victory.

The second week we see Samuel obeying God and answering His call. His obedience to God is a wonderful example of how God blesses us when we are obedient to what He wants us to do. Jonah was not. He disobeyed God and what a price he had to pay.

Joy is so clear in her description of the mind.

Satan is after our mind. But he is the loser. She explains so clearly how we can give our mind and heart to God and defeat Satan. She tells us about some of the hearts of some of God's choice servants in His Word: Esther, Job, David, Lydia, and Paul.

We can repair any heart damage that we might have, such as, deceitfulness, waywardness, and brokenness.

We can be restored. Thank God.

Joy gives us God's call on all of our lives the last week of this Bible Study. We are to rejoice, even through trials. This final week we see that we will even rejoice more when the trials are over if we rejoice going through the trials. We have to choose to believe or not believe when we go through trials.

We are to obey, and in doing so serve Him. When we do these things we will have a Victor's Cry.

I see so many people going through such hard times in these days we are living in. Everyone seems to be going through something. And I see many being attacked in their area of ministry to God. I see pastors who have illness and are not able to preach for awhile. Singers who are not able to sing for Him because of throat problems. Musicians who are not able to play an instrument in services because of hand problems. Scripture says that the devil is a roaring lion seeking whom he may devour. But he is a loser. We are victorious in Christ. And no matter what we are going through, we will have a Victor's Cry.

—Beverly Lowry

WEEK ONE

Living out God's Promises

Day One: Abraham's Belief

Today's Bible Reading: Genesis 12, 15, 18:1-15
Today's Banner: Genesis 15:1b, "I am your shield, your exceedingly great reward."

God promised Abraham that he would be the father of many nations and that his descendants would number as the stars in the sky (Genesis 15:5). In Genesis 17:8 God told Abraham, "I will give unto thee, and to thy seed after thee, the land wherein thou art a stranger, all the land of Canaan, for an everlasting possession; and I will be their God."

The promise began with Abraham; it was delivered through Moses' guidance in the wilderness and Joshua's leadership into the Promised Land. Abraham believed the promise with faith. Moses saw the promise in action, and Joshua experienced the promise. Abraham had to leave his country. His love for God motivated a life of pure devotion to the God of Israel. What would have happened if Abraham had not obeyed and believed the promise God had given? <u>Abraham would have missed the greatest blessing of his life.</u>

Has there ever been a time when unbelief caused you to miss a great blessing or when your belief gave you a wonderful blessing?

_____

_____

_____

In Genesis 12, we meet Abraham and his family. Our introduction begins with God telling Abraham to go. Go where? God told Abraham to go, and God would give the details later. If you are like me, I prefer the details first. My husband, Gene, knows very well that I do not like surprises. For me, knowing ahead of time does not ruin the surprise. Personally, I would have struggled with just being told to go and not having the details.

Abraham was obedient and went. When Abraham was told he would be the father of many, he believed the Lord. Abraham was old and Sarah was beyond childbearing years. In fact, when Abraham told Sarah the Lord's promise she did not believe and sent him to have a child with Hagar, the handmaid. Oh, the generations of problems that could have been avoided if Sarah would have believed and if Abraham had not allowed Sarah to influence his obedience. Our lives are filled with choices, and our choices have consequences.

1. According to Genesis 16:11-12 what was the result of Abraham allowing Sarah to influence his belief in what God had promised?

   _____
   _____
   _____

2. Has there ever been a time when you have allowed someone else's opinion and influence to sway you to doubt God?

   _____
   _____
   _____

There may be times when God is telling you to go and serve Him in a particular area. Due to circumstances you may ask others to pray for you and the decision you must make. I believe in the power of prayer. When you seek counsel, be careful not to let human counsel take the place of God's direction. We can easily be swayed by the opinions of others. How often do we let others influence our obedience to God? I think this is what we see with Abraham and Sarah.

Loving God with our mind may be the most important trait. The mind is where our thoughts begin that can have the power to sway our hearts. The choices we make are eventually made by seeds planted in our mind.

Living out God's Promises

Regardless of Abraham and Sarah's choices, belief or unbelief, God is not capable of breaking His promises. At the age of ninety-nine—thirteen years later—God told Abraham that Sarah would have a child. Once again, Sarah did not believe. Genesis 18:9-14 gives the account of Sarah's unbelief.

Write a brief summary of Genesis 18:9-14.

___

When God tells us to go yet we remain where we are because the details are not in place, we shortchange ourselves in our spiritual journey. Let's not be so detail oriented that we miss the greatest adventure of our lives.

Where is God asking you to go?

___

Is there something He is asking you to do?

___

What, if anything, is keeping you from obeying His call?

___

What promise has God given you that you need to claim?

_____
_____
_____

Pray a prayer thanking the Lord for His promise on your life and ask Him for strength to live out His promise.

_____
_____
_____

Day Two: Sarah's Joy

Today's Bible Reading: Genesis 21:1-6
Today's Banner: Genesis 21:6a, "God has made me laugh."

According to Sarah, Abraham believed a bogus promise. She was probably thinking, At his age, he's hearing things. She knows that physically it was impossible for her to conceive, much less give birth. She began to influence his disobedience with the facts of their age and her physical impossibility. Once the shadow of doubt was cast on Abraham's belief there was room for Satan to work.

Have you ever experienced a time when the facts were in direct opposition of your faith?

_____
_____
_____

The Lord always has an answer to our unbelief and lack of faith. The Lord in Genesis 18:14 (NKJV) answers the unbelief, "Is anything too hard for the LORD? At the appointed time I will return to you, according to the time of life, and Sarah shall have a son." Our unbelief does not determine if God will keep His promise. It only determines to what extent we will experience His promises.

Guess what. Sarah had a son and named him Isaac, just as Abraham had been told. At some point, Sarah believed the promise, definitely by the time labor pains had begun. We find Sarah laughing again in Genesis 21:6. The first time Sarah laughed was with sarcasm (Genesis 18:12). The second time God caused her to laugh out of a joyful spirit. When you obey God, believing He will do what He promises, your heart will overflow with joy. True joy comes from an obedient spirit. When God asks you to do something that in your finite mind seems impossible, you will find the greatest joy.

Can't you just imagine the looks at the first Lamaze class that Sarah attended when the other women realized she wasn't someone's mother-in-law there for support but was herself, a mother-to-be? In those nine months did Sarah keep to herself? Did she feel the need to try to explain her pregnancy? Each time that she gazed down at her expanded tummy, was she in awe of the miracle that God had performed? Daily, she was reminded that the Lord God Jehovah keeps His promises. How many hymns of praise did she and Abraham sing as they looked into the starry sky?

I can't imagine all the emotions that Sarah must have felt over the course of those nine months. It is only fitting that the moment that baby boy was laid in her arms he was named in accordance with a jubilant emotion. Isaac means laughing one. Don't you know there was great laughter and tears of joy the day little Isaac arrived.

Don't you know every time she looked at Isaac her spirit would whisper with deep gratitude, thanking the Lord for His promise? I'm sure if Bill Gaither had been there to video the birth we would hear Gloria singing, "You are a promise. You are a possibility. You are a promise with a capital P…"

Experiencing God's promises for our lives brings inexplicable joy. God has given us many promises in His Word.

Jeremiah 29:11,13, "For I know the thoughts that I think toward you, says the Lord, thoughts of _____ and not of _____, to give you a _____ and a _____ . And you will _____ Me and _____ Me, when you _____ for Me with _____ your heart."

Jeremiah 33:3, "_____ to Me, and I will _____ you, and show you _____ and _____ things which you do not know."

What is keeping you from claiming God's promises for your life?

_____

_____

Are you laughing with sarcasm rooted in unbelief?

_____

_____

Are you filled with joy over the promises God has given you?

_____

_____

What promises has God spoken to your heart? Have you claimed it?

_____

_____

Day Three: Abraham's Obedience

Today's Bible Reading: Genesis 22:1-19
Today's Banner: Genesis 22:1b, "Here I am."

Obedience can be difficult. If you are as strong willed as I am, you understand this difficulty even better. No matter your temperament, we all struggle with obedience some time or another. Nevertheless, God tested Abraham's belief. Unbeknownst to Abraham, God had enrolled him in Obedience 401. This time not only would Abraham's love for God be tested, but his love for his only son would be tested, too.

What was God's command to Abraham in Genesis 22:2?

_____

_____

If we are going to love God with all of our soul, it has to be done holding nothing back. In Abraham's case, this meant his only son. This was the son that God had promised, the one who would be the beginning of generations that would make Abraham the Father of a great nation. Every hope and every dream rested on Isaac. God had fulfilled His promise. Now He was giving the ultimate test.

In Genesis 22:5 we can see that Abraham's faith had not been shaken.

What does Abraham say in verse 5?

_____

_____

_____

Abraham calmly tells his servants that they are to stay with the donkey. He and Isaac will go to Mt. Moriah. While they are there they will worship, and they will return. If God were asking you to give up your most precious possession, would you still worship Him? Could you still worship Him?

I heard Max Lucado say, "The greatest form of worship is obedience." Abraham walked up that mountain with wood and his son Isaac. He was ready and willing to worship because he had brought an obedient spirit to the altar of sacrifice. The sacrifice would take everything he had but the worship would be life changing. Life can be so good, and the things in our life can be so enjoyable that those things can easily become gods. Was this test from God to Abraham to see if the Lord God Jehovah still had first place?

Write Exodus 34:14.

_____

_____

_____

We serve a jealous God who wants all of our hearts, all of our souls, all of our minds, and all of our strength. I truly believe that it took all of Abraham's heart, soul, mind, and strength to carry out the Lord's command that day. From the beginning of time God has stressed obedience.

Match the scripture reference with the verse:

- A. Mark 4:41   ___His commandments are not burdensome
- B. Luke 11:28   ___The doers of the law will be justified
- C. John 14:15   ___The wind and the sea obey Him
- D. Romans 2:13   ___We know Him if we keep His commands
- E. 1 John 5:3   ___Blessed are those who hear the word of God and keep it
- F. 1 John 2:3   ___If you love me, keep my commandments

There are many more verses dealing with the subject of obedience. I hope this gives you some idea of the importance of obedience in our lives. If David had obeyed the Seventh Commandment, his life would have been much more peaceful. If Moses had obeyed and spoken to the rock instead of striking it with his rod as God had instructed him, Moses would have been able to experience the Promised Land. There are illustration after illustration in the Bible of what happens when disobedience rules the heart and when obedience has first priority.

Has there been a time in your life when the consequence of disobedience was unbearable or you remember the absolute delight you experienced when you chose to obey?

_____

_____

_____

Abraham was able to obey the Lord's command no matter the cost because He trusted with a surrendered heart. I have heard preachers say that Abraham believed God so much that even if he had sacrificed his son that day God would have raised Isaac from the dead. Abraham believed, trusted, and worshiped the God of the impossible.

Genesis 22:15-18 tells that Abraham's obedience was blessed by God. We sometimes like to place the word *consequence* in a negative context. There are consequences when we obey. For Abraham his consequence was blessing. His descendants would multiply as the stars of the heaven; they would be victorious over their enemies…all because he obeyed. Just think, our obedience to the Lord affects future generations.

Day Four: Isaac's Trust

Today's Bible Reading: Genesis 22:6-10
Today's Banner: Hebrews 12:29, "For our God is a consuming fire."

Isaac asked the most obvious question: "Where is the lamb for the burnt offering?" When an Israelite offered a burnt offering, there were specific requirements. First of all, the animal that would be sacrificed had to be a male without blemish. Second, none of the sacrifice was to be eaten. It was to be completely burnt, totally consumed by the fire. Third, the individual making the sacrifice could do this of his own free will.

Living out God's Promises

Knowing what we know about burnt offerings, when Abraham bound Isaac and laid him on the altar, Isaac probably knew what was coming. He understood that he was about to be killed and consumed with fire and that this was of his father's free will. According to the Scriptures, Isaac never questioned, never doubted, and did not struggle. He only trusted.

Write the order of events that day.

Gen. 22:6 _____

Gen. 22:7 _____

Gen. 22:8 _____

Gen. 22:9 _____

Gen. 22:10 _____

Gen. 22:11 _____

Gen. 22:12 _____

Gen. 22:13 _____

Gen. 22:14 _____

Isaac is one of those people that I can't wait to meet. I want to hear him recall that day's events. I wonder if Isaac breathed a sigh of relief when the angel of the Lord spoke and told Abraham not to kill his son. I want to know how long they worshiped the Lord, Jehovah-jirah, after the ram had been provided for the burnt offering.

Write Romans 12:1.

_____

_____

_____

Isaac trusted his father as he lay on the altar. Do you trust your Heavenly Father? Are you willing to offer yourself at your own free will as a living sacrifice? Are you willing to be totally consumed by His refining fire? Can you say as Job, "When He has tested me, I shall come forth as gold" (Job 23:10)?

Abraham taught his son a priceless lesson that day. Nothing came between him and God. God possessed all of Abraham. Isaac knew his father was sold out to the Lord. Because of his father's commitment to God, Isaac's trust in Abraham was not difficult even when his life was in question. When we live a sold-out life, others are affected.

Is there anything in your life that you have put before God? If so, confess it now and give God His rightful place in your life–first place.

_____

_____

_____

Day Five: Right Choices

Today's Reading: Hebrews 11:23-27
Today's Banner: Joshua 24:15a, "Choose for yourselves this day whom you will serve."

My former pastor, Bill Park, preached a series of messages on "Making the Right Choices." In one of his sermons he made the statement that *a man's character is broadcast by the choices he makes.* As we have studied the life of Abraham, I think we can safely conclude that his right choices broadcast a character of righteousness.

Unlike Abraham, Moses' life is recorded from infancy to death. Moses, the future leader of the Israelites, would rescue them from slavery, but only after a life-changing choice was made.

Hebrews 11:24-26 tells us, "By _____, Moses, when he became of age, _____ to be called the son of Pharaoh's daughter, _____ rather to suffer affliction with the people of God than to _____ the passing pleasures of sin. _____ the reproach of Christ _____ riches than the _____ in Egypt; for he looked to the _____."

Our First Lady Eleanor Roosevelt said it well when she spoke of the importance of choice. "One's philosophy is not best expressed in words. It is expressed in the choices one makes. In the long run, we shape our lives, and we shape ourselves. The process never ends until we die. And the choices we make are ultimately our own responsibility." The day that Moses made the choice to walk out of the palace and the lifestyle that it offered was the beginning of God's shaping him to be the great leader that he would one day become.

Living out God's Promises

Moses chose to reject the world's prestige. (vs. 24)
He chose to reject the world's pleasure. (vs. 25)
He chose to reject the world's pressure. (vs. 27)

We are told to do the same in 1 John 2:15-17: "Do not love _____ _____. If any one loves the world the love of _____ _____. For all that is in the world—the _____ of the flesh, the lust of the _____, and the _____ –is not of the Father but is of the world. And the world is passing away and the lust of it; but he who does the _____ _____ of God abides _____."

Bill Park said in a sermon that we must recognize that when a child of God is making choices in any way of personal godliness, Satan attacks that choice before, during, and after the choice is made. Satan moves into high gear when the choice for godliness is being acted upon. The right choice does not mean the easy choice.

In Hebrews 11:26 we see the weight of Moses' decision. In the NKJV verse 26 begins with the word *esteeming*. This word means to weigh the decision out. I don't think Moses just woke up one morning and decided to pack his bags and leave. I believe God began to reveal Himself to Moses and a greater purpose for his life. Over time, Moses' longing to be in God's will was greater than all the comforts the palace offered.

Have you come to a place in your life that you desire God's will above anything else?

_____
_____
_____

Verse 27 states that Moses forsook or abandoned Egypt. When the choice is made to follow God, everything else has to be completely abandoned. Not only did Moses abandon Egypt that had held him and his people captive, but he allowed himself to be used of God to set His people free.

Write 2 Timothy 1:7.

_____
_____
_____

Is fear keeping you in the comfortable palace, just out of reach of God's will?

What are you afraid of? _____

Who do you fear? _____

Moses made the right choice. He made the choice to abandon Egypt. He made the choice to look to the One He could not see rather than fear the king he could see. When the choice to serve God comes there are times that fear is the first enemy to be defeated. Don't make the choice of indecision because fear seems like a giant. Make the choice to do what God has for your life. God will conquer the enemy of fear.

Claim Exodus 14:13-14: "Do not be afraid, (your name) _____. Stand still and see the salvation of the Lord, which He will accomplish for you today. For the Egyptians (write your fear) _____ whom you see today, you shall see again no more forever. The Lord will fight for you, (your name) _____, and you shall hold your peace."

Life is full of choices. Choices have consequences. Make the right choices.

—Bill Park

WEEK TWO

Effective Obedience

DAY ONE: WHEN GOD CALLS

Today's Reading: 1 Samuel 1:20–3:18
Today's Banner: John 10:3b "…He calls His own sheep by name."

As you begin, I think it is important to understand what brought Samuel to the place where God would call out his name. We will find Samuel's journey in these first three chapters unique because of the lifestyle which he lived.

Samuel's name means _____ (1 Sam. 1:20)

Samuel is dedicated "as long as he lives he shall _____ (1 Sam. 1:28)

Samuel ministered to _____ (1 Sam. 2:11)

Samuel ministered before the Lord wearing a _____ (1 Sam. 2:18)

This will be a sign in one day your sons will _____ (1 Sam. 2:34)

I will raise up for Myself a faithful _____ (1 Sam. 2:35)

The Word of the Lord was _____ (1 Sam. 3:1)

The Lord called _____ (1 Sam. 3:4)

Samuel ran to _____ and said _____ (1 Sam. 3:5)

The Lord called yet again,_____ So Samuel went to _____ (1 Sam. 3:6)

The Lord called _____ he arose and went to _____ (1 Sam. 3:8)

Eli said to Samuel _____ (1 Sam. 3:9)

The Lord came; Samuel answered _____ (1 Sam. 3:10)

"It is the Lord, Let _____ (1 Sam. 3:18)

Samuel had a different life as far back as he could remember. Samuel had a rich heritage. His mother believed in the power of prayer. It was her prayer that God heard and answered with a baby boy. Samuel also had a first-hand experience of what it meant keeping one's commitment to the Lord. His mother had promised the Lord that she would give up her child to Him if he would honor her request to have a baby. I can't begin to imagine what it would be like to literally "give up" my child, knowing I would only see him one time a year. At a young age, Samuel understood the power of prayer and true commitment and was learning to serve. Now Samuel was about to learn what it was like to have a personal encounter with the Living God.

God called Samuel because God had a ministry that took the integrity of someone like Samuel. After God called to Samuel we don't hear from Samuel again until 1 Samuel 7:3.

Samuel spoke to Israel saying, "If you return to the Lord with all your hearts then put away _____... and prepare _____ and _____; and He will deliver you from the Philistines."

Samuel lead Israel in prayer (vs. 5) then to repentance (vs.6), and God's reward was given to Israel (vs.10-11)

Samuel tells Israel on three different occasions to "serve the Lord with all your heart." In chapter 7 Samuel gives the command after the Israelites asked for and got the king they wanted. The third time we find this command is in 1 Samuel 12:24. Samuel is reminding God's people of the great things God has done for them.

God will not wake you in the middle of the night with His audible voice like he did for Samuel, but He does call. He calls us to prayer, to commune with Him. He calls us to repentance. He calls us to victory.

When God calls you, will you know His voice? God still speaks. We need to be still and listen.

Effective Obedience

Psalm 95:7

_____

_____

_____

John 10:3

_____

_____

_____

John 10:27

_____

_____

_____

Our Shepherd calls us by name, just as He did Samuel. Our Shepherd knows us. God called Samuel to a great ministry. Samuel was Israel's constant reminder that the God of Israel was alive and well. Each time Samuel gave the command to serve the Lord with all their heart Israel was in need of repentance. They had wandered. Each time, the God of Abraham accepted their sacrifice, heard their repentance, and gave His forgiveness.

No matter what you have done or where you are, God is calling you to love Him with all your heart, with all your soul, with all your mind, and with all your strength. As Samuel said so long ago to a weary people, "Only fear the Lord, and serve Him with all your heart; for consider what great things He has done for you." Considering all of that, embrace the life God is calling you to. Answer His call.

1 Samuel 12:21 "And do not turn aside, _(your name)_____; for then you would go after empty things which cannot profit or deliver, for they are nothing."

Day Two: Ocean Revival

Today's Reading: Jonah 1-4
Today's Banner: Hebrews 13:5b, "I will never leave you nor forsake you."

Jonah's life is a great example of a judgmental spirit that affected his obedience to Christ and ultimately affected his ministry. The story of Jonah opens with God's commanding Jonah to go to Nineveh and tell them of their wickedness. In verse 3 we find Jonah running. There isn't even a dialogue between Jonah and the Lord. God said, "Go," and Jonah got up and left. It is interesting that twice in verse 3 it is stated he left the presence of the Lord. If you have been saved for any length of time there is probably a Tarshish in your life. I can remember a specific time in my life where I ran to "Tarshish" and left the presence of the Lord. I was defiant. I made the choice to disobey the Lord.

Do you have a Tarshish experience in your life?   Yes.   No.

First of all, we find Jonah making the choice to disobey. We know he heard the Lord's command because he disobeyed. Disobedience doesn't just happen. We know what the Lord has asked of us. We have taken time to think about it, and then we must make a choice: obey or disobey.

The second most interesting aspect found in verse 3 is Jonah found a ship going to Tarshish. Misery loves company. When wrong choices are made it will be easy to find others to travel with. Jonah didn't find a boat going to Tarshish. He found a ship. When the choice is made to flee the presence of the Lord, company will be found. He was welcomed aboard.

I can imagine Jonah getting on the ship and introducing himself to a few of the other men. They patted him on the back and treated him like he was one of them. Jonah settled in, found his place, and probably jumped right in to a game of cards. The laughter came easy. He truly thought he was among friends. The others thought Jonah was one of them. The world will always welcome a wayward child of God because for a brief moment it appears their way is right.

Before he boarded the ship he did something that at the time seemed the norm. He paid the fare. Whenever we make the choice in our mind to disobey the Lord and then we act on that decision, there will always be a price to pay. I'm sure the initial fare was not expensive. The true expense of our journey into disobedience comes over time.

Jonah paid the price for the trip, and he boarded the ship. Take notice of how he boarded this ship. The Bible states he went down into it. The journey of disobedience is always a downward spiral. That may be why disobedience, in the beginning, can be so easy.

My husband and I love to hike. As cruel as the climb up a mountain can be I anticipate the view we will see when we get to the top. I will admit I find the trip down the most enjoyable because it is the easiest. As easy as the hike down may be, I feel a twinge

Effective Obedience

of disappointment because the adventure is over. I am so thankful that in our spiritual journey if the decision has been made to disobey and we find ourselves on that downward spiral, Grace and Mercy are there to meet us at the bottom. We may flee the presence of the Lord, but He never leaves nor forsakes us.

Write Hebrews 13:5b.

_____

_____

_____

God sent a storm to awaken Jonah's spirit. The storm came and affected everyone near Jonah. Our disobedience does affect others. The storm was meant for Jonah but it brought fear to all those around him.

Where was Jonah during the storm?

_____

Many times when we choose to disobey and continue on the path of rebellion, our spirit becomes numb. In the beginning of our disobedience, the Lord may send small things into our lives to get our attention. A storm at sea was nothing unusual. Yet the intensity of this storm was cause for fear. Storms will come in our life. As I have heard many times, "You are either in the midst of a storm, coming out of a storm, or headed into a storm."

A storm in your life does not always mean there is sin present in your life. I have known godly people to go through storms, and I have wondered why. But in Jonah's case, the storm was a result of his sin. It has been my experience that if a storm came into my life as a result of my sin the storm was much more intense.

If you are truly the Lord's, He will do whatever it takes to bring you back. The storm brought enough fear to bring on a confession from Jonah. He admitted his disobedience to the others on the ship (1:7-10). The storm brought confession, but the fish brought repentance. Jonah 2:1-10 is a repentant heart praying to an Almighty God. Jonah's prayer went from despair (vs. 1-3) to acknowledging his sin (vs. 4-8) to thanksgiving (vs. 9-10).

When the choice is there to obey or disobey God's calling and the wrong choice is made, I am forever grateful that we serve a God of second chances. Jonah 3:1, "And the word of the Lord came unto Jonah the second time." There was no hesitation this time. Jonah knew that whatever awaited him in Nineveh could not be worse than his experience in the belly of a fish.

Jonah still hadn't learned everything God wanted to teach him. He repented of his sin, obeyed God's calling and went to Nineveh. He delivered God's message to the people of Nineveh, and the people repented. God forgave and showed mercy on this wicked city.

Then we find Jonah was unhappy with the results. At first he wouldn't go to Nineveh because of their wickedness, and he was afraid of what they would do to him. In chapter 4, Jonah was angry. He was upset because God spared the people of Nineveh.

How often do we sit in judgment and watch to see what God is going to do to someone else because of their sin? Yet, if we would take a long, hard look at our own life we would see where God gave mercy and granted grace instead of judgment. Jonah's attitude was as if he had done God a favor by preaching in Nineveh and now God had Jonah's permission to destroy the city and the people therein. A judgmental attitude is a weakness in the Christian's armor. Satan knows if he can tempt us with judgmental thoughts toward others and those thoughts take root, our ministry will be ineffective.

Write a prayer of thanksgiving to the God of second chances and if you need to, confess your judgmental attitude.

_____

_____

_____

_____

_____

_____

Day Three: The First Kings Bed and Breakfast

Today's Bible Reading: 1 Kings 17: 8-24
Today's Banner: 1 Corinthians 10:31b, "whatever you do, do all to the glory of God."

The story of Elijah and the widow intrigues me. What a great example of patience, obedience, and the reward of service. This story sets a standard for service. First of all, don't ever assume someone is too old, too fragile, or incapable of serving.

Effective Obedience

This story begins with an interesting statement.

What does God tell Elijah in 1 Kings 17:9?

_____

_____

_____

When God saves us I truly believe that the ability and desire to serve Him is given the moment we are born into the family of God. Secondly, God places other believers in our life to lead us in ministry. The irony is when Elijah obeyed and went to Zaraphath and approached this woman and asked for bread, she never said no but gave a grand excuse.

Have you ever given excuses for not serving?   Yes.   No.

Explain.

_____

_____

_____

Can't you picture it? Elijah sees her gathering sticks, and God lets him know that this is the widow He had told him about. Elijah asks her for water. Notice she had no problem giving him water, after all water is free, there is little effort involved. The moment Elijah asked for bread, the excuse came. What an excuse!

What did the widow tell Elijah was the reason she could not bring bread? (vs. 12)

_____

_____

_____

I am not sure how I would respond if I went to someone and asked him to help out with something and basically was told no because he was going home to die. Elijah probably thought that he had heard God wrong or that he had the wrong person. I would love to have seen the look on Elijah's face.

This lady had the tools and the ingredients to make the bread, yet she told him she had no bread. Remember she had no problem giving the water–no effort. Suddenly, work was involved, and she wasn't able to give. After all, she was going home to die. People are struggling to thrive spiritually because they won't give what God is asking for.

Elijah's persistence paid off. I chuckle because Elijah did not get caught up in her pity party. He basically said, Go ahead and go home and die, but before you do that make me some bread first. (vs. 13) Then came the hope and the promise.

What is the promise given to the widow in verse 14?

___

When we begin to meet the needs of others, our needs are met. This truth has stood the test of time. What a story she had to tell. I can see it now. She baked for the neighbors, cooked meals for the sick, and was the first to volunteer to bake the cake for parties. She had something to give. She had a reason to live! God rewarded her obedience.

The Lord gives exactly what we need when He asks us to serve Him. He will give strength to sustain us. He will give the energy needed for the task at hand. He will give joy unspeakable. What a story we will have to tell!

Elijah wasn't sent to this woman just to ask for bread. He was sent to this woman to encourage, give hope, and give her a reason to live. Isn't it interesting that Elijah first asked for water. Jesus is the Living Water. We can draw from a well that never goes dry.

Write John 4:14.

___

Second, Elijah asked for bread. Jesus is the Bread of Life. When we eat from the Bread of Life our souls will never go hungry.

Write John 6:35.

_____

_____

_____

He is our all in all. He is our sustainer. He is our hope, and He is our promise. If you are weary in His service, take heart. Drink from the Living Water and eat of the Bread of Life. Let Him sustain you. If you are caught up in your own pity party, lift up your head. It is not God's will that you struggle spiritually. You can live a vivacious life for the Lord. Find a ministry and put forth some effort. You will find that you will have enough to give–no more, no less. God will sustain you and give you what you need to serve Him in whatever ministry He calls you to.

God desires for us to obey Him. Love Him with all your strength.

Day Four: One's Heart Cry

Today's Bible Reading: 1 Samuel 1:1-19; 2:1-10
Today's Banner: Psalm 62:8b, "God is a refuge for us."

Hannah had a tender heart toward the Lord. Her desire to have a child was so great that it was her primary request when praying to the Lord. She was one of Elkanah's two wives. The other wife, Peninnah, was able to have children and was cruel to Hannah. Every year they would travel to the temple to sacrifice and worship.

What does 1 Samuel 1:4-5 tell us about Elkanah's love for Hannah?

"But to Hannah he would give a _____.

I can't imagine a more sensitive matter than not being able to have children, much less having the other wife provoking me and making me miserable all because I could not have children. All I can say is, What a lady. As far as we know, she did not retaliate. She did cry. She did not eat, and her heart ached within her soul (vs. 7-10). Even with all of that, she knew the one thing she must do: pray. Her prayer was with such great emotion that Eli thought she was drunk. There have been times that I prayed with great earnest but no one ever thought I was drunk. Her prayer matched her desperation that day.

What follows is quite remarkable when you think about it. Eli saw Hannah and thought she was drunk. He reprimanded her and told her to put away the wine. Hannah was quick to tell him that she was not drunk. She had not been drinking anything; she was pouring everything out before the Lord.

Are we truly empty of ourselves so that the Lord can give us our request?

Psalm 142:2

_____
_____
_____

Psalm 62:8

_____
_____
_____

God had Hannah right where He wanted her, empty of herself. We can see in the above verses that Hannah wasn't the only one who poured out her soul to the Lord. David had learned to do that. God knew the child Hannah was to have, but He needed Hannah to be the mother Samuel needed. If Hannah was empty of herself then she would have nothing to depend on but the Lord.

Eli then told her to go in peace and the God of Israel grant you your petition which you have asked of Him (vs. 17). The Bible tells us that she went her way, ate, and her face was no longer sad. God heard her heart's cry. She conceived Samuel, and she carried out her commitment. Once he was weaned she took him to Eli and said, "For this child I prayed, and the Lord has granted me my petition which I asked of Him. Therefore I also have lent him to the Lord; as long as he lives he shall be lent to the Lord" (I Samuel 1:28).

Hannah had poured out her heart. Hannah kept her promise to the Lord. Hannah rejoiced at God's goodness. In chapter 2 we find that Hannah's heart cry had turned into her heart song. When we pour out our hearts to God no matter the circumstance, He hears our cry. The trial may be unbearable for a season but he promises that joy comes in the morning (Psalm 30:5).

Hannah rejoiced in_____ (vs. 1)

Hannah smiled _____ (vs. 1)

Effective Obedience

In verse 2 Hannah learned what about God _____

The Lord is the God of _____ (vs. 3)

In verse 4b Hannah rejoices that those who _____ are girded with _____

Who has been made feeble? _____ (vs. 5b)

Hannah rejoices for she has experienced that the God she serves: (verse 6-8)

Kills and makes _____

Brings _____ and brings _____

Makes poor and _____

He brings _____ and _____

He raises _____

He lifts_____

...All this to set them among princes and make them inherit the throne of glory. Hallelujah! We serve an awesome God! Hannah had been emptied of herself and God had poured into her His joy unspeakable.

Write a prayer to the Lord pouring out to Him your heart's cry and receive His filling of unspeakable joy.

_____
_____
_____
_____
_____
_____

Day Five: Total Surrender

Today's Bible Reading: Judges 13:1-25–16:1-31
Today's banner: John 3:30, "He must increase, but I must decrease."

Bruce Larson, in *Believe and Belong*, tells how he helped people struggling with surrender: "For many years I worked in New York City and counseled at my office any number of people who were wrestling with the yes-or-no decision. Often I would suggest they walk with me from my office down to the RCA Building on Fifth Avenue. In the entrance of that building is a gigantic statue of Atlas, a beautifully-proportioned man who, with all his muscles straining, is holding the world upon his shoulders. There he is, the most powerfully-built man in the world, and he can barely stand up under this burden. 'Now that's one way to live,' he would point out to his companion, 'trying to carry the world on your shoulders. But now come across the street with me.' On the other side of Fifth Avenue is Saint Patrick's Cathedral, and there behind the high altar is a little shrine of the boy Jesus, perhaps eight or nine years old, and with no effort he is holding the world in one hand. My point was illustrated graphically."

Richard A. Hassler said it so well, "We have a choice. We can carry the world on our shoulders, or we can say, 'I give up, Lord; here's my life. I give you my world, the whole world.'"

Have you surrendered everything to the Lord? Are you still trying to carry the weight of your world on your shoulders? Samuel heard God's voice and answered the call. Is God calling you and asking you to surrender your life to His ministry?

_____

_____

_____

Maybe you identified with Jonah. God is calling you to go and be the light to someone else. You are afraid to speak to him/her about Christ. Instead of surrendering to His call and obeying, you have decided to disobey the Lord in this area. Total surrender for Jonah meant going somewhere that was not comfortable. Yet, Jonah found that choosing what he would and would not surrender is not as comfortable as he thought it would be.

Who is God asking you to share His love with? _____

Elijah experienced delight in his surrender. His willingness to reach out to another allowed the Lord to work wonders in the widow's life. When Hannah surrendered her most precious gift, the Lord blessed her with more children, and an entire nation was touched through the ministry of Samuel.

Effective Obedience

One of the most powerful illustrations that I have heard and demonstrated is very simple. Close both your hands and make a fist with each hand as if you were holding on to something very tightly. Now, picture in your mind the Lord is standing before you wanting to give you something. You cannot receive His blessing because your hands are holding tight to other things. The only way you can receive what the Lord has is to open your hands and let go of what you are holding on to. When you hold on to what you have and all that makes up your world, you cannot be open to receive the blessings the Lord wants to give you. Now, open your hands with your palms facing up. The Lord is there ready to give you His blessings and you are able to receive what He has for you.

Are you ready to let go of your things and let God give what He has for you? What are you holding that is difficult for you to let go of?

_____

_____

Don't be as Samson was, God called him to a life fully devoted to Him, yet Samson's sinful desires caused him to abandon the life God had planned and ended in imprisonment and death.

Luke 6:38, "_____ and it will be _____ to you: good measure, pressed down, shaken together and _____ will be put into your bosom. For with the same measure that you use, it will be measured _____ to you."

Luke 11:9, "So I say to you, _____, and it will be _____ to you; seek and you will _____; knock, and it will be _____ to you."

The Lord desires to give us more than you can imagine. He asks that you give Him one thing: your life. He desires all of your heart, all of your soul, all of your mind, and all of your strength. You will find when you surrender completely to the Lord, you will live a life of rejoicing, not regret. Your life will be abundant, not lacking anything.

Write Ephesians 3:20.

_____

_____

_____

As Jim Elliot said, "He is no fool who gives what he cannot keep to gain what he cannot lose." Can you say the same? Open up your hands and give God your family, your job, your ministry. Give Him your life and see what He will give in return. Surrender everything to Him.

Lord, I give you

_____

_____

_____

_____

_____

_____

WEEK THREE

All of My Mind

DAY ONE: UNDERSTANDING THE BATTLE PLAN

Today's Bible Reading: Psalm 46
Today's Banner: Psalm 46:1a, "God is our refuge and strength."

"Love the Lord with all your mind" (Luke 10:27). I am convinced; the mind is where the battle begins. Isaiah 26:3 gives a great foundation for building a ready defense against the enemy: "Thou wilt keep him in perfect peace, whose mind is stayed on Thee." The New Living Translation states it this way: "You will keep in perfect peace all who trust in you, whose thoughts are fixed on You!" This is the first stone on which to sharpen your sword.

I believe there are four parts to the enemy's plan to wear us down mentally. First, doubting what God can do. The second is worry: can I trust in the Lord? Next, insecurity can paralyze us spiritually. Last but not least, pride has the ability to devastate us spiritually. Believe me, the enemy has a strategy! He plans his work on the believer, and he works his plan. We, too, are equipped with a plan. To execute God's plan for victory we have to study the strategy, God's Word.

Deuteronomy 20:3, "Do not let your _____ faint, do not be _____."

2 Samuel 22:40, "You have armed me with _____ for the battle _____."

Psalm 24:8, "The Lord _____ and _____, the Lord mighty in _____."

The Victor's Cry

Psalm 46:1, "God is our _____ and _____."

Psalm 59:9b, "For God is my _____."

Isaiah 40:29, "He gives power to the _____... He increases _____."

Isaiah 41:10a, "_____ , for I am with you."

Philippians 4:13, " I can do all things through _____ who _____ me."

From the moment Adam and Eve bit into the fruit in the Garden of Eden, the battle for your soul has been raging. Once God sent Christ to be the sacrifice for your sins and you accepted His free gift of salvation, Satan knew he would never conquer your soul, but he could fight you, fatigue you, and discourage your every effort to live in victory.

In the days of the Old Testament when the Israelites would go into battle, they would carry a banner. A banner was much like a flag. It was usually carried at the head of the military band to indicate the line or march or the rallying point.

Psalm 60:4, "You have given a _____ to those who fear You. That it may be _____ because of the truth."

Psalm 20:5, "And in the name of the Lord we will set up _____."

Exodus 17:15, "And Moses built an altar and called its name, _____."

Isaiah 11:10, "And in that day there shall be a Root of Jesse, Who shall _____ _____; for the Gentiles shall seek Him, and His resting place shall be glorious."

Jesus Christ is our Banner! Just as it was prophesied in Isaiah that Jesus Christ would become our banner. The banner was lifted up for all to see the day that the Son of God was crucified. The Banner stands alive and well rallying us to be more than conquerors. The war was won at the resurrection. Death has been defeated. Sin has been destroyed through the blood of Jesus Christ. We have Jesus Christ—our banner—to take into every battle we fight.

Not only has God given us the strength to fight, He has given us the Banner of Truth to carry with us. Our personal responsibility required for protection is our armor. Soldiers are given the protective gear to fight, but it is the soldier's responsibility to put it on and wear correctly. What is our armor?

Ephesians 6:11-15, "Put on the whole _____, that you may be able to_____."

Satan's wiles are the devil's schemes or tactics. Satan has a plan that he is carrying out to keep us from living victoriously. I like the way The New Living Translation words this verse.

1 Peter 5:8, "Be careful! Watch out for attacks from the devil, your great enemy. He prowls around like a roaring lion looking for some victim to devour." As a mighty warrior we need to dress for success.

First, we need to put on the _____. (Eph.6:14a)

John 8:32 tells us that "you shall know the truth and the truth shall make you free." If you want to come out of the battle a victor you must fight with truth.

The _____ of righteousness (vs. 14b) is there to protect our heart. Christ is the only one who can make us righteous. Second Corinthians 5:21 tells us that "He made Him who knew no sin to be sin for us, that we might become the righteousness of God in Him."

Ephesians 6:15 says, "Our feet covered with the gospel _____."

The gospel of Jesus Christ is about reconciling man to God, making peace.

Romans 5:10 states that when we were _____ we were _____ to God through the death of His Son, much more being reconciled, we shall be saved by his life.

In verse 17 we are told to put on the _____ and the _____ which is the word of God.

According to verse 16, the most important part of our armor is our Shield of ____.

It is the part of the soldier's armor that will be able to quench all the fiery darts of Satan. Isn't it interesting that we can fight with righteousness, truth, the gospel, our salvation, and the Word of God, but without our shield of faith the enemy can still get to us? Satan can bring up our past and briefly we will forget our righteousness in Christ Jesus. The wicked one can plant false thoughts and feelings that have the potential to make the truth seem fuzzy. The great deceiver can tempt us to doubt our salvation and the life change the gospel of peace brings. The devil can tell us that we are too busy and make life seem so chaotic that making a priority to spend time in God's Word seems impossible. Yet Satan knows that if we take up our shield of faith, he has nothing.

Match the following reference with the scripture

    _____ 1. Matthew 17:20   a. Your faith should be in the power of God.

    _____ 2. Romans 1:17   b. Walk by faith, not by sight.

    _____ 3. 1 Corinthians 2:5   c. If you have faith as a mustard seed.

    _____ 4. 2 Corinthians 5:7   d. The just shall live by faith.

Dear friend, as we step on the battlefield, we will find only time has changed. The battle has been the same through the ages. Put on the armor of God and "Fight the good fight, lay hold on eternal life…" (1 Tim. 6:12a).

Carry your banner high.

Day Two: The Battle of Doubt

Today's Bible Reading: John 20:24-29
Today's Banner: Proverbs 3:5, "Trust in the Lord with all your heart."

For some, doubt can be the easiest weapon Satan uses against them. I don't know about you but at some point after I received Christ as my Savior, doubt set in. The doubt usually would come after I had done something I knew to be wrong. I could hear Satan say (not audibly), If you were really a Christian you would not have done or said that. Then the guilt would set in and I would ask for forgiveness, knowing full well that God had forgiven me to remember my sin no more (1 John 1:9).

At times the guilt would still linger even after I had made things right, only to return to doubt from the thoughts of "What if I wasn't forgiven? What if I really never got saved?" Someone may be reading this, and you know exactly what I am saying. The Battle of Doubt is your fight, and you just can't seem to win. You know full well Satan's plan because you see it in action in your life. There is hope! Let's pick up the weapon that is sharper than any two-edged sword.

Hebrews 4:12, "For the Word of God is _____ and _____ and _____ than any two-edged sword, piercing even to the division of the _____ and _____

_____, and of joints and marrow, and is a discerner of _____ and _____ of the heart."

I like the Message version of this verse: "God means what he says. What He says goes. His powerful Word is sharp as a surgeon's scalpel, cutting through everything, whether doubt or defense, laying us open to listen and obey."

Wow! Did you read that? His powerful word can cut through doubt! I like that this verse also states that what God says goes. There are times when my children ask "Why?" and my answer at times is, "Because I said so." That is basically what God is telling us here. We can quote scripture to Satan and the demons, and they have to flee because God said so. God is God. There is no one like Jehovah!

When you're in the Battle of Doubt you have a mighty sword. You have a strategy that has passed the test of time: God's Word. Memorizing scripture wasn't something I had a choice in when I was growing up. I attended a Christian school, AWANA, and then a Bible college. Therefore, I memorized Bible verses whether I wanted to or not. I am thankful that I was given that opportunity. Some of you may not have had that same opportunity. Whatever the reason, scripture memorization is vital to fighting the good fight.

What is the strategy to winning the Battle of Doubt? The opposite of doubt is certainty and confidence.

Isaiah 30:15, "In quietness and _____ shall be your strength."

Proverbs 3:26, "For the _____ will your confidence."

Hebrews 3:6b (NLT), "Remain _____ in our hope in _____."

For some, the Battle of Doubt is not over security about who they are in Christ. It is in the everyday things of life: marriage, parenting, service. Let's talk about your ability to serve. You feel the Holy Spirit's tug on your heart to serve in a ministry at your church. There you are in the corner of the arena, and Satan is in his corner. The bell rings and you freeze because Satan comes out swinging doubts of capability, competence, and the final blow comes when he says, "They wouldn't want you."

You walk away and kick yourself all the way home that you didn't speak up and volunteer. The defeat of doubt is unbearable. You try to bandage your wounds with the calming influence of excuses. There will be plenty of other people that will help out with that, you tell yourself. "After all, I have never done that before." I mean, heaven forbid we try something new to further the gospel.

In your relationships, do you doubt that God can revive a dead relationship, bring your spouse to salvation, and restore a broken relationship? Whatever your case may be, God can.

Exodus 3:14 God tells us who He is: "_____ Who _____."

I AM is the rebuilder, restorer, and I AM can break down walls that have brought separation and isolation to your soul. The great I AM can overshadow doubt and give strength to your soul. Just as Moses doubted in the wilderness what God was asking him to do. God promised to go before him. Moses went from doubt to confidence in what God could do. He saw God deliver His people and destroy the Egyptians. I say to you as Moses said to God's people, "See the salvation of the Lord, which He will accomplish for you today."

Be confident in God's work in your life and all that makes up your life. God is working to make you His workmanship. Don't allow Satan's tactic of doubt to slow down the progress. Memorize and claim Philippians 1:6 for your life.

Write Philippians 1:6.

_____

_____

_____

Carry your banner high. Conquer the Battle of Doubt.

Day Three: The War on Worry

Today's Bible Reading: John 11:1-44
Today's Banner: Colossians 3:15, "Let the peace of God rule in your hearts."

Some of you have not spent much time on the battleground of doubt, but you are too familiar with the war on worry. You try but you can't even take a break from the fight. You are weary. You live in the ditches of discouragement and want desperately to taste victory. When I think of worry I think of Martha. Poor Martha, she has always gotten a bad rap, but she was a worrier. Jesus was coming to visit, and she was worrying and fretting over the house and the meal. She worried herself right into frustration.

She was frustrated because Mary was sitting at the feet of Jesus. Martha could not enjoy the company of God Himself because worry had taken root in her life. Worry was her ticket to frustration and complaining. Later in the Scriptures, Martha makes her dramatic appearance again when Lazaras, her brother, dies. I don't mean to disrespect the dead but Martha's worry causes me to chuckle.

Lazaras has been sick, and Mary and Martha sent word to Jesus that their brother was very ill. I am sure Martha thought that surely Jesus would come immediately and heal her brother. After all, the Messiah had spent time in their home and eaten her cooking. As the days passed, I can see Martha pacing, wringing her hands, and wondering, Where is Jesus? She was worried sick that Jesus had not received the message. Maybe He did not understand the immediate need. What were they going to do? Their dearest Friend has the ability to make the blind to see, the lame to walk, and to raise the dead, but He did not come when they needed him most. All Martha could think was, Where is Jesus?

The search committee was in place and the maps had been passed out highlighting all the possible places He and His disciples could be when someone said that Jesus had been seen coming in to town. Relief! Finally, Jesus was here, but it was four days too late. Martha ran to meet him and immediately exhaled her worry with blame. John 11:21 (NKJV) says that Martha said unto Jesus, "Lord, if you had been here, my brother would not have died."

Basically, Martha was saying, I have worried about my brother, and he died, and then I worried about you. Why didn't you come? I worried that something had happened to you. I have been worried sick. I've been trying to hold the family together, take care of the burial arrangements, and keep up with all the guests that came to grieve with us and who brought what dish. Where have you been?

Then she quickly adds a side note, "But I know, that even now, whatsoever thou wilt ask of God, God will give it thee." A response like this is so true for the person who fights worry. Energy is wasted while you worry if things will work out as you think they should, yet when it is all over the response is, I knew you would pull through for me, God.

At the tomb, Christ asked for the stone to be taken away. Once again, Martha, not quite sure the Lord can handle this on His own (After all, He was four days late.) informed Him that Lazaras stank because he has been dead four days. Can't you just picture it? Jesus was standing in front of the grave, Mary on one side trusting her Savior, Martha on His other side holding her nose, as a crowd of friends watched with anticipation to see what Jesus will do. Martha basically said, You know, Lord, I believe you can raise my brother from the dead, but what in the world are you going to do about that smell?

Even though we have viewed Martha from a humorous viewpoint, we can all relate. She believed Him to do the impossible but not the practical. When I am fighting the War on Worry, I will ask myself, Why is it you have no trouble trusting the Creator of the universe with your soul but wonder if He will provide this particular need?

What is it you are worried about? _____

How do we fight to win this war? We fight with truth, God's Word. The strength for the victory is found in trust. Trusting God will overpower worry.

Proverbs 12:25 says "_____ in the heart of man causes depression, but a good word makes it glad."

The NLT tells us "worry weighs a person down…" Christ understands your struggle with worry.

Matthew 6:25-34 tells you not to worry about your _____ (vs.25), your _____ (vs. 28) and do not worry about _____ (vs. 34).

In Philippians 4:6, Paul reinforces what Christ stated in Matthew. Paul gives us the strategy to win the war on worry: "Be anxious for nothing" The NLT states it this way, "Don't worry about anything; instead pray about everything." Tell God what you need and thank Him for all He has done and is doing." The simplicity of this truth is almost too good to be true.

I like the way this verse ends by encouraging us to thank the Lord for all He has done for us already. I have found that when I start thinking of all the things God has done for me I find my anxious feelings begin to subside. About two weeks before I gave birth to our second child, my husband was laid off from his job.

We were not anxious for two reasons: We had seen the lay-off coming because the company was downsizing, so it did not surprise us when his name was on the list. We had money in savings and felt sure that would help get us through until he found a job. Our son was born and was about two weeks old when we noticed the car wasn't running like it should. Gene took it in to have the engine checked and came home with bad news. The engine would need to be replaced. I cried.

Blame it on the hormones, but I was worried. This would take a chunk out of our savings. What were we going to do? My husband gently reminded me that God had provided our every need thus far, He would provide for this. I knew he was right. The engine was repaired, and we never went without one single thing we needed for the next six months.

We learned the weapon most useful in the Battle of Doubt is confidence in the Lord. Prayer is the weapon of choice to win the war on worry. Pray. Such a small word, but when put into action it can pack a punch.

Paul was a great example of not worrying and praying about everything. After all, every time he turned around he was in a prison. Worry could have stifled his style of preaching. Instead he set out to preach the gospel and let God take care of the details. Don't you know that the next time he was put in jail (after he had gotten out of jail due to an earthquake God sent) Paul had a great prayer of remembrance and thankfulness? Just imagine what Paul's prayer might have been: "Lord, here I am in Cell 14 and am concerned about the mice and the sanitation, but I am thankful You placed me here to reach other souls for You. I would not have had the opportunity to preach Christ here if I had not been arrested. I know You have my best interest in mind and in Your timing will get me out of here. The earthquake was exciting, and You really showed Yourself last time I was put in prison. Even the jailor and his family believed. Whether You use another earthquake or just quietly set me free, I trust You will come through." Prayer gives us strength for today, whereas worry robs us of what we need for today.

When I focus on the good things God has done for me—and believe me His track record cannot be matched—I find it more difficult to worry about how He is going to take care of the present. I am not minimizing Paul's imprisonment or Martha's sorrow. Paul's confidence in the Lord increased, and Martha's war on worry ended. Paul knew that God will always come through even in the toughest situations, and Martha learned that God is always on time.

Thank God for His provisions for you.

Confess your worry, write a prayer of your trust in the Lord and claim 1 Peter 5:7:

_____

_____

_____

Claim His promises. Be victorious. Choose your banner so the Enemy knows you will not be defeated.

Day Four: The Landmine of Insecurity

Today's Bible Reading: Psalm 31:1-24
Today's Banner: Psalm 31:3, "You are my rock and my fortress."

How many of us find ourselves on the frontlines of this battle? Webster's dictionary tells us that insecurity is uncertain, not protected, unsafe, loose, shaky, and not highly stable. I will never forget when I worked with Severely Emotionally Disturbed children after I graduated from college, we were asked to participate in Ropes Course Training. The first two days of our training was uneventful, and then we had to put the classroom lectures into practice. It was time to tie on the ropes and the safety harness and climb. I am not afraid of heights as long as I feel safe and secure. As a child I loved climbing trees, but I always made sure there was a strong limb I could hold on to. The types of climbs I had took me to a certain point where there was nothing to hold on to, my rope and harness were all that would catch me if I fell. Those few seconds would seem like forever. What was the point in that training? First, it was to help us understand the type of insecurity the kids were experiencing, secondly it taught that in the midst of our feeling shaky and unstable, there was always the rope to hold on to.

When do you feel uncertain? What makes you feel uncertain?

_____

_____

_____

"The man with one watch knows what time it is. A man with two watches is never sure." (source unknown) Luke 16:13 reminds us that "No servant can _____ two _____; for either he will hate the one and _____ the other, or else he will be _____ to the one and _____ the other. You cannot serve God and mammon."

Remember the shield of faith that we are given to take into the battle. If you are uncertain about God's promises then you are easily swayed, therefore your faith is weakened. Do you know someone who has the most difficult time making up his mind? I usually can make a decision quickly, but I have been trying to decide what color to paint our living room for two months. I cannot decide; therefore the living room has not been painted. That is exactly what indecision does. When you make the decision to be indecisive you get nowhere.

Is there something in your life causing you to feel unstable or unprotected?

_____

_____

_____

Maybe you are facing a situation that has you wondering where God's protection is.

Second Samuel 22:3 (NKJV) says, "The God of my _____ in whom I will _____; my _____ and the horn of my salvation, my _____ and my _____, My Savior, you save me from violence."

Just as I would climb thirty to forty feet to learn the techniques during that ropes course, if I focused on my instability and the vulnerability that I felt, I would be quick to freeze. Instead I learned I had to focus on the security of the harness and the strength of the one holding the rope below.

Any battlefields we find ourselves on are filled with landmines waiting to explode with insecurity to paralyze us, mangle us, and leave us to doubt the security of the next step. Maybe you are thinking, I step on those landmines everyday, and I feel so defeated and worthless to the army of the Lord.

Psalm 4:8, "I will both lie down in _____ and sleep; For You alone, O Lord, make me to _____."

Do you need rest from your insecurities? Carry your shield of faith and stand firm in your decisions to trust the Lord. He promises to give rest.

Exodus 33:14, "And He said, 'My _____ will go with you, and I will give you _____.'"

In Matthew 11:28 the Savior beckons you. "Come unto Me all you who labor and I will give you _____."

I learned to trust the rope when my feet were dangling, and there was nothing to grab hold of. Not only did I learn to trust the rope, I learned to trust the person holding the rope. My security did not come in what I could hold on to; my security came in what was holding me. My friend, the Living God is holding you. You may be dangling and grappling for something to hold on to, rest in the secure arms of the Almighty. As you learn to trust, you will see the landmine of insecurity and be able to sidestep Satan's attacks.

Lift your banner high and win this battle.

Day Five: The Destruction of Pride

Today's Bible Reading: 2 Kings 5:1-14
Today's Banner: Isaiah 42:8, "I am the Lord, that is My name; And My glory I will not give to another, Nor My praise to carved images."

Pride is the enemy that has the sneak attack strategy and can be difficult to detect. Pride can camouflage in the best of intentions, in the most sincere Christians, and be in the midst of ministry. Pride thrives off of blending in. Making one think that it belongs is the strategy pride depends on to win the war. We can fight and successfully claim the victory in many battles but if pride gets a foothold in the Christian's camp then the battle ultimately has been lost.

Pride is the enemy that has many disguises. Pride can appear as anger, contempt, oppression, deceit, presumption, self-will, stubbornness, or strife. This great enemy has several characteristics such as condemnation, lust of the eyes, lust of the flesh, or the pride of life. Shame always has pride's back, making sure the attacks are deliberate and debilitating.

Shame comes behind pride and pours out its poison of debasement, destruction, rejection of God's Word, and a persecuting spirit. Pride is successful when the mind is hardened and one is overcome with self-deception. Pride can find its way into the Christian camp through self-righteousness, unsanctified knowledge, inexperience, or possession of power and wealth. Satan knows that pride can hinder the Christian from growing in Christ. Pride can also hinder the desire to seek God wholeheartedly. When Satan wins the Battle of Pride, one's testimony can be damaged.

As my high school basketball coach would often say, "The best offense is a good defense." I say the same to you. Let's familiarize ourselves with pride's strategy and battle plan to destroy us. As stated earlier, pride wears many different styles: anger, contempt, oppression, deceit, presumption, self-will, stubbornness, or strife. How is anger connected to pride?

Who was Naaman? (vs1) _____

Who waited on Naaman's wife? (vs. 3) _____

Where was the young girl from? (vs. 4) _____

Who was the prophet Naaman sent for? (vs. 5-9) _____

Did Elisha personally deliver the message to Naaman? (vs. 10) _____

What was the first thing that made Naaman so angry? (vs. 11) _____

_____

What was the second reason Naaman became angry? (vs.12) _____

_____

What was the servant's response? (vs. 13) _____

What did Naaman do to be healed? (vs. 14) _____

What was Naaman's response? (vs. 15) _____

_____

Naaman thought very highly of himself. So much so that he would rather be eaten with leprosy than get wet in the Jordan River. How many of us refuse healing because it would require humility? Naaman wanted the easy way out. He wanted Elisha to come in person, wave his hand, and the leprosy disappear. When there is something in your life that is eating away at your spiritual health, we want God to meet us in person, wave His hand, and the problem be gone. So many times, God requires our humility to gain the health.

Isaiah 57:15, "The High and Lofty one who inhabits eternity, whose name is Holy: I dwell in the high and holy place with him who has a _____ and _____ spirit, To revive the spirit of the _____ and revive the heart of the _____ ones." God wants to revive us, heal us and see us walk in His holiness.

James 4:6, "God resists the _____ but gives _____ to the _____."

James 4:10, "_____ yourselves in the sight of the Lord, and He will _____ _____ you up."

Naaman was told to go down to the Jordan River and dip seven times. If he had to dip then he had to lower himself. Once Naaman got himself out of the picture, God could work a miracle.

Are you angry because things are not going your way? Do you need to get yourself out of the picture and humble yourself before the Lord?

_____

_____

_____

Not only did Naaman get angry when God did not heal him the way Naaman thought he should, Naaman became angry then stubborn. When you are the commander of the army of the King of Syria stubbornness can be a great strength. But on this day, stubbornness was his greatest obstacle. Naaman struggled with not being in command. Naaman had to take a command from a servant, God's servant. Stubborn means not easily controlled. Naaman was used to being in control. Now he needed to be controlled in order to be well.

You want to be healed? Submit to God's authority. Why is that when fighting pride we are so easily controlled by the one who wants to harm us, and we struggle with the One who can set us free? Maybe because getting you out of the way and letting God have the glory and control of you can be the battle of a lifetime.

Is there anything that you are not giving over to God's control?

_____

_____

_____

Does stubbornness have a stronghold on your soul and a grip on your life? Listen closely to the servant who (I'm sure with great fear) approached his commander in verse 13 "…if the prophet had told you to do something great, would you not have done it? How much more then, when he says to, 'Wash and be clean'?" If Naaman had needed to do something grand then it would have still been all about Naaman. When God heals it can only be all about Him. Pride says, "It's all about you." Humility proclaims, "It is all about God."

Where in your life is it all about you?

Proverbs 13:10, "By _____ comes nothing but strife."

Proverbs 16:18, "Pride goes _____ destruction…"

Daniel 5:20, "His [Nebuchadnezzar's] spirit was _____ in _____."

Win the Battle of Pride with a humble and contrite heart. Don't give the great deceiver the victory. Shout your victor's cry giving all the glory to God. Let Isaiah 42:8 be the banner you carry into the Battle of Pride.

WEEK FOUR

All of My Heart

Day One: Esther's Bold Heart

Today's Bible Reading: Esther 1-2, 4, 8
Today's Banner: Acts 2:28, "You have made known to me the ways of life; You will make me full of joy in Your presence."

I love the story of Esther's life. What woman wouldn't? There's a Cinderella in all of us. We love the stories of the young Prince looking for his princess, finding her and living happily ever after. Esther's life did not resemble Cinderella, but she did become queen. She experienced true royalty. We know several things about Esther's childhood. She was an orphan and her cousin Mordecai raised her. She was beautiful. The most important fact about Esther is that she was Jewish.

King Ahasuerus put out a decree to bring all the beautiful young women to his palace. He was looking for a new queen. Esther found favor immediately from Hegai. Esther was given beauty preparations besides the ones that were already planned to be given (2:8-9). She was also given seven choice maidservants from the king's palace. When it was her turn to go into the king, it wasn't long before she found favor in his sight, and he chose Esther to replace Queen Vashti.

As the story goes, there was a conspiracy to destroy the Jews. This plot was orchestrated by Haman. Haman was the top dog in the palace. His authority was right beneath that of the king (Esther 3:1-2). Mordecai discovers the plot and gets word to his cousin, Queen Esther. For Esther to reveal the plot to the king, she would have to put herself in a vulnerable position with the king. It was their custom that no one could appear before the king unless he had summoned them. If anyone went in to the king without being called by him, it was certain death (Esther 4:11).

I love Mordecai's firm but gentle plea. First, he reminds Esther that if the decree goes out and all the Jews are killed, what makes her think she will escape death? He reminds her of her heritage: she is a Jew also. Then he says the famous words from this great story, "Yet who knows whether you have come to the kingdom for such a time as this" (Esther 4:14).

God may have you in the places you are for such a time as this. Esther found favor in the sight of the king and he stretched out his golden scepter to her (Esther 8:3-7). God was faithful to Esther and His people. Esther had a great petition to put before the king, and it could have cost her life.

I find it interesting that throughout the book of Esther God's name is never mentioned, but His providence is woven throughout Esther's life, Mordecai's life, and a generation of Jewish people. Providence means divine guidance or care. Provident means making provisions for the future.

God's providence would have been more difficult to see had Esther not had a willing heart. There was boldness in Esther that I think surprised her. She had to do the one thing that was forbidden, approach the king without an invitation. She had to tell him who she truly was: a Jew. She also had to expose his most trusted individual that roamed the palace: Haman. She would either be doomed to death or delivered from it.

As much as I love the story of Esther, I am so glad that I don't have to approach my King with fear and trembling. You are a daughter of the King. Show Him your willing heart. Approach the throne.

Hebrews 4:16, "Let us therefore come _____ to the throne of grace, that we may obtain _____ and find _____ to help in time of need."

Ephesians 3:12, "We have _____ and access with _____ through faith in Him."

God desires to make provisions for your future. He wants to daily guide and care for you. We do not have to wait for Him to hold out a scepter before we can approach Him. Tragedy doesn't have to take place before we come and kneel at his throne. Desperation shouldn't be our motivator to come into His presence. He says, "Come boldly."

What is keeping you from approaching the King of kings?

He has a life of royalty planned for you, a future and a hope. As you approach the King today, know that He wants to give you the very best. He desires that you live a full life. He accepts you as you are. He knows your past. Let Him give you a glorious future.

The Jews were spared destruction all because someone approached the throne with boldness. Satan desperately wants to bring destruction into your life, but as long as he knows you have accessibility and you daily approach the King of kings, he is limited.

Esther 8:15 says that Mordecai went out from the presence of the king in royal apparel. The city was glad. Do others know that you have been in the presence of the King? Just as the Jews had light, gladness, joy, and honor; God wants all of that and more for you.

Psalm 100:2, "Serve the Lord with _____; Come before His _____ with singing."

Psalm 16:11, "You will show me the path of life; in your _____ is fullness of _____; At your right hand are pleasures forevermore."

Psalm 91:15, "He shall _____ upon Me, and I will _____ him; I will _____ him and _____ him."

Run into His presence and worship. Be bold. Hold high the banner and shout to the enemy.

Day Two: Job's Confident Heart

Today's Bible Reading: Job 1-2, 26
Today's Banner: Job 19:25, "I know my Redeemer Lives."

Are you confident in who God is? Do you have confidence that He never changes? Write out the promise given in Hebrews 13:8.

_____

_____

_____

The book of Job is an incredible story about an incredible man. Job was a wealthy man. Job 1:3 tells us that he was the greatest (wealthiest) of all the people of the East. Job's story begins with the telling of his character. What four descriptions are you given in Job 1:1?

The Victor's Cry

1. _____
2. _____
3. _____
4. _____

Job not only had impeccable character, he wanted that for his children. Job prayed for his children and offered burnt sacrifices for them.

Read Job 1:4-5 and explain why Job offered burnt sacrifices for his children.

_____
_____
_____

Job had the good life. Others looked at him and may have thought, He has it all, but Job's friends weren't the only ones watching Job. The Lord had watched Job. When Satan came into the Lord's presence, it is God who bragged on His servant Job.

How does Satan respond to the Lord? (1:9-11)

_____
_____
_____

What is the Lord's reply to Satan in verse 12?

_____
_____
_____

In one day, Job lost everything. I cannot imagine losing all that I own, my source of income, and my children in a twenty-four-hour period. If Job lived today and experienced the same loss, he would be the Breaking News, the Headline News, and the front page of the newspaper. His tragedy would be the talk of everyone. I'm sure everyone was talking about Job's tragedy.

If you lost everything you owned, your source of income, and all your children how do you think you would respond?

_____
_____
_____

Job 1:20-22 tells us how Job responded. Write Job's response.

_____
_____
_____

Job understood God's sovereignty. Sovereignty means supreme in power; chief, highest, having independent authority. God answers to no one. He has independent authority to do as He wills with creation.

Write Psalm 50:1.

_____
_____
_____

1 Timothy 6:14-15 says, "You keep this commandment without spot, blameless until our Lord Jesus Christ's appearing, which he will manifest in His own time, He who is the _____ and only _____, the _____ and Lord of lords."

This was the God that Job understood, served, and worshiped. God had supreme authority in Job's life, and Job submitted.
Not only did Job have confidence in God's sovereignty, he had confidence in God's goodness.

What was Job's reply (Job 2:10b) to his wife after she told him to "curse God and die"?

___

___

___

After losing everything, would you still have confidence in God's goodness?

Exodus 34:6, "The Lord God, merciful and gracious, longsuffering and abounding in _____ and truth."

Psalm 23:6, "Surely _____ and mercy shall follow me all the days of my life."

Psalm 27:13, "I would have lost heart, unless I had believed that I would see the _____ of the Lord in the land of the living."

Psalm 52:1, "The _____ of God endures _____."

Psalm 107:8, "Oh that men would give thanks to the Lord for His _____."

Write Romans 2:4.

___

___

___

So far, you have seen that Job had confidence in God's sovereignty and His goodness. In Job 9 Job shows his confidence in the Lord's omniscience.

What does Job say in 9:4? "God is _____ in heart and mighty in strength."

Job 12:13, "With Him are _____ and strength, He has counsel and_____."

Job had an understanding and respect for the all-knowing, all-powerful God. God places us in situations or trials, mountaintops and valleys because His omniscience can see that each season of our life will need one or the other to provide a way for His glory to be seen. In chapter 19 Job proclaims his Redeemer. After losing it all (from a human viewpoint) and his three friends had kicked him while he was down, Job gives one of the greatest proclamations.

Job 19:25 proclaims "For I know my Redeemer lives." What a proclamation that is!

When you can shout from the rooftops while surrounded by utter failure (from the world's standards) that you know your Redeemer lives, Satan must flee. No destruction, despair, or desolation can hold a stick to your comfort and confidence that comes in the name of the Lord.

Job knew that when He could not see God or find Him, he could have absolute confidence in God's omnipresence. Job says in 23:10,

"But He _____ the way that I _____; when He has tested me, _____ shall come forth as _____.

Job understood that it is not up to us to see God or find Him in the darkest hour. Have confidence that God knows exactly where you are, and He will not take His eyes off of you.

Psalm 34:15, "The eyes of the Lord are on the _____."

Proverbs 5:21, "The ways of man are before the _____."

Proverbs 15:3, "The _____ are in every place."

Job had confidence in who God is because Job understood the majesty of the Almighty. In Job 26 God's majesty is acknowledged. Job saw God over his circumstances instead of the circumstance over God. I believe that as long as you keep your eyes on God and who He is, the circumstances of life dim in the light of His majesty. Who is God and what has He done to show us His majesty?

Job 26:7, "He hangs the earth on _____."

Job 26:8, "He binds up the _____ in His thick clouds, yet the clouds are not _____ under it."

Job 26:10, "He _____ a circular _____ on the face of the waters."

Job 26:12a, "He _____ up the sea with His _____."

Job 26:12b, "By His _____ He breaks up the _____."

Job 26:13, "By His _____ He adorned the Heavens."

Job ends this chapter saying all of this and "these are the mere edges of His ways." God has only shown us a small display of His majesty, but what He has shown cannot be denied and not always explained, but calls out that your Redeemer lives.

God displays His majesty and declares His wisdom. Job walked a path that few can understand. From the world's eyes, Job's journey took him from greatness to failure, from wealth to poverty, from health to disease, from joy to grief. The journey that God took Job on took him from good to great, riches to richer, from wellness to health, and from content to unspeakable joy. In this trial Job learned that God establishes a weight for the wind. He made a law for the rain and a path for the lightning bolt. If God will do all of this for nature, He wants to do above and beyond with you and me. Job learned that God prepared wisdom and made a way to have it.

Job 28:28, "The _____ of the Lord, that is wisdom, and to _____ from _____ is understanding."

Do you have confidence in the Lord? Do you trust God's omnipotence (power), omniscience (knowledge), omnipresence (presence), sovereignty (authority) and goodness in your life? Can you say as Job did in 42:2, "I know that You (God) can do everything, and that no purpose of Yours can be withheld from You."

Day Three: David's Tender Heart

Today's Bible Reading: 2 Samuel 7, 9, 12:1-23
Today's Banner: Psalm 51:8a, "Make me hear joy and gladness."

David is probably one of the most if not the most-loved person written about in the Bible. (Obviously Jesus Christ is the most loved, but you know what I mean.) I think many of us like to read about David and hear about David because we can identify with something that David experienced. If I had to use one word to describe David it would be tender. David was tenderhearted. Maybe this tenderness came naturally or maybe it was cultivated in the fields while tending sheep. Whatever it was, that tenderness grew and God saw it.

All of My Heart

David is first seen in the fields. All of Jesse's sons were at the sacrifice that Samuel was offering except David. Samuel was there to choose the next king over Israel. God was not impressed with any of Jesse's sons, but He made it clear when David was brought to the sacrifice that he was the one to be Israel's king. The Lord reminded Samuel that he was not to "look on the outward appearance…the Lord looks on the heart."

David was tender to God's instruction. In 2 Samuel 7:5, God makes a covenant with David. What does the Lord ask David to do for Him? _____

How long had it been since the Lord had dwelled in a house (vs. 6)? _____

The Lord reminded David from whence he had come. He was a shepherd in the sheepfold and now he was ruler over God's people. Your past does have influence on your present relationship with God and the things that God may ask you to do. David understood the importance of having shelter and a gathering place for sheep. Sheep need security. Sheep need to be kept safe and kept together. Does God need a house to dwell in? Of course He does not. But He knows that we need a gathering place and shelter.

What is in your past that God is using for His glory now that you are His child and serving Him?

_____

_____

_____

David wrote in Psalm 84:4, "Blessed are those that dwell in Your house; they will be praising You."

David had a tender heart toward others. How we treat other people is a good indicator of where our heart is. In 2 Samuel 9 David asked if there was anyone left of the house of Saul, that David may show him kindness for Jonathan's sake. Jonathan was David's dearest and closest friend. If you have ever been so fortunate as to find a Jonathan Friendship, count your blessings. Ziba, David's servant, told David that one of Jonathan's sons lived in Lo Debar and he was lame. David wasn't interested in his physical condition, for he desired a relationship.

What does 2 Samuel 9:6-13 tell us about the relationship of Mephibosheth and David?

1. _____
2. _____
3. _____
4. _____
5. _____
6. _____

David knew to look past the imperfections and see the need. How many times do you see someone's faults and that hinders you from seeing the need? Mephibosheth's relationship with David did not cure the handicap, but I can assure you that David's friendship changed Mephibosheth as a man. When you reach out to someone and show tenderness, you have the ability to change a life.

David's tenderness toward God's rebuke amazes me. David had such a strong love for the Lord that when he had sinned, David's heart could not stay hardened very long. Second Samuel 12 is the end of the story about David's adulterous affair with Bathsheba. Nathan the prophet had been sent by God to confront David about his sin. Nathan painted a beautiful word picture about two families and their sheep (2 Samuel 12:1-7). David understood Nathan's story and was led to repentance.

Are you tender to God's rebuke?   Yes.   No.   Sometimes.

Explain.

_____
_____
_____

David was forgiven but he paid the consequences for his sin. In verse 14 Nathan tells David that his sin has given great occasion to the enemies. When you harden your heart and choose to sin, even if for a little while, you open the door wide for the Enemy to attack.

After the confrontation had taken place, then the death of the child which he and Bathsheba had conceived, where was David? (vs. 20) _____

All of My Heart

Did he say the Lord was not fair? Did he hide himself because of shame? Did he put away the crown and go back to the sheepfold? No. David worshiped. My friend, do not let sin keep you from your loving Father. Confess it, and let God's forgiveness flow into your life.

Psalm 32 is a psalm about the joy of forgiveness.

What does David say in verse 1? "_____ is he whose transgression (sin) is _____."

(vs. 5) "I acknowledged my _____ to You, and my iniquity I have not _____."

(vs7) "You are my _____ place; You shall _____ me from trouble; You shall surround me with songs of _____."

David's prayer is recorded in Psalm 51. Maybe you need to pray this prayer today and confess sin, for you desire a tender heart toward the things of the Lord.

Write verse 10.

_____

_____

_____

In verse 8 does David ask the Lord to cause him to feel shame and guilt? _____

What does David ask the Lord to make him hear? _____

You read in verses 12-17 that David asks God to:

Restore what? _____

Uphold with? _____

Deliver from? _____

Open what? _____

When your heart is tender you can walk in the joy, restoration, praise, and confidence in the Lord's forgiveness.

Write 1 John 1:9.

_____

_____

_____

Carry your banner high in the face of the Enemy when he tries to overpower you with guilt and shame because of your past sin.

Day Four: Lydia's Open Heart

Today's Bible Reading: Acts 16: 13-15
Today's Banner: 2 Timothy 4:2a, "Be ready in season and out of season."

Few things are known about Lydia. We do know that she sold expensive purple cloth. She heard the message of Timothy, Paul, and Silas. She opened her heart and paid attention to all that Paul spoke of.

Write the order of events found in verses 13-15.

_____

_____

_____

First of all, we should never underestimate the power of conversation. Paul, Timothy, and Silas did not preach to these women. They sat down and talked with them. The message of Christ was presented in a non-threatening way. We don't know what they spoke about, but it was significant enough that it caught her attention.

Is your conversation such that when others listen they are drawn to Christ?

Colossians 4:6 says, Let your _____ always be with _____, seasoned with _____ that you may know how you ought to answer each one."

I like the way the New Living Translation says it: "Let our conversation be gracious and effective…"

Lydia was a business woman. Purple cloth was expensive, and those who sold it did well for themselves. Paul, Silas, and Timothy did not let her wealth discourage them from speaking. You should speak about the Lord no matter who is listening. Never assume a person's financial status makes them different in how you approach them with Christ's salvation.

Lydia was open to what was spoken that day, and it led her to salvation and baptism. Her entire household was saved and baptized. Lydia's salvation led to her hospitable attitude. Maybe that was the spiritual gift she was given. I do not know. Whatever the case, she was not going to take no for an answer.

What did Lydia say to Paul and the others in verse 15?

_____

_____

_____

When God changes someone's life, it is important that godly relationships are established.

Can you recall those first relationships that were established after you became a Christian? Maybe you were saved at a young age. Recall the godly relationships God has placed in your life.

_____

_____

_____

I wonder how many times Paul and the others visited with Lydia and her family after that day. When Paul, Timothy, and Silas talked with those women that day down by the riverside, someone listened. A life was changed. One conversation changed many lives for all eternity. Let us be cautious in our conversation. Let us be deliberate to speak of God's goodness and saving grace every chance we get. Make a point to establish relationships with new believers and other sisters in Christ.

Presenting the salvation message is not a three-step plan that can only be done at the end of a sermon. Your speech should be sprinkled with the things God has done for you. Speak up; you never know who is listening and the life that will be changed because you testified of God's goodness. End today praying for someone you need to begin talking with, that they will come to know Christ.

Day Five: Paul's Peaceful Heart

Today's Bible Reading: Galatians 5:16-26
Today's Banner: Isaiah 9:6, "His name shall be called Prince of Peace."

Paul had not always been at peace with himself and with God. Before Paul became a follower of Christ, he was known as Saul. Saul persecuted Christians. He sought out those who proclaimed Jesus Christ as the Son of the Living God and the only way to the Father. Paul's life changed on the road to Damascus, and the journey thereafter was anything but dull.

Even with the persecution Paul faced and the many times he was put in jail for preaching the gospel, his life was peaceful. Your life in Christ is more peaceful in the midst of trials than it would be outside of Christ without trials.

Romans 5:1, "Therefore having been justified by faith, we have _____ with God through our _____."

Peace comes first through a relationship with Jesus Christ. Salvation will not solve your problems but it will give you the relationship with the person who has the solution.

Paul calls us to live a life of peace. You are to be a peace-seeker, peacekeeper, and peacemaker. Galatians 5:22 gives the fruit of the spirit.

What is the fruit of the Spirit? _____

We are to bear the fruit of peace. What ways can you bear the fruit of peace?

_____

_____

_____

Not only do we find peace through Jesus Christ, but Jesus Christ is peace.

Write Ephesians 2:14.

_____

_____

_____

When Christ comes into our lives, the Prince of Peace can break down the wall of discord. Walls have a purpose and can be healthy if built around relationships with the purpose to maintain health and safety. If a wall is built in the middle of a relationship, Christ is no longer the center of that relationship. Instead the wall becomes the focal point rather than Christ.

Are you building a wall in the middle of your relationships or is Christ the center?

_____

_____

_____

If Christ is peace and Christ is the center of all you do and are, then you will have peace.

Are you experiencing peace in your life? If not, why not?

_____

_____

_____

The peace of God guards your heart and mind, Philippians 4:7 tells us. When you experience the peace that cannot be explained, your soul and mind reap the benefits. Has there ever been a time that you could not explain the peace you had in the midst of a circumstance?

_____

_____

_____

Colossians 3:15 tells us to "let the _____ of God _____ in your heart." The day and time we live in can be anything but peaceful. Watch the evening news and you could be convinced the world will come to an end within the hour. Peace can be difficult to find.

If peace comes through a relationship with Jesus Christ and Jesus Christ is peace, then who should be ruling our hearts? _____

John 14:27, "_____ I leave with you, My _____ I give to you; not as the world gives do I give to you. Let not your heart be _____, neither let it be afraid."

Peace will guard your heart. Peace should rule our heart. What is your responsibility?

Write 2 Timothy 2:22.

_____
_____
_____

If you pursued peace how would that change your life and the lives of others?

_____
_____
_____

Paul had his taste of life where peace with others was hard to find. I cannot imagine living a life that consisted of seeking out others for the purpose of having them persecuted and sometimes killed, all because of something they believed. That is the life he had before he met Christ. It is fitting that Paul is the one to write and encourage us to live in peace with others.

Write Romans 12:18.

_____
_____
_____

Satan wants to bring disorder and mayhem to your spirit. Whoever or whatever brings turmoil to your life, let peace rule in your heart and let peace guard your heart. Allow the Prince of Peace to break down the wall that desperately wants to divide. Carry your banner with boldness. Show the Enemy that he cannot take your peace.

WEEK FIVE

Heart Repair

DAY ONE: THE DECEITFUL HEART

Today's Bible Reading: Psalm 43
Today's Banner: John 17:17, "Your word is truth."

We are commanded to love God with all of our hearts, but if we give place to deceit then our devotion to God is greatly diminished. Some of the definitions given for deceit or to deceive are to trick, practicing deceit, misleading, to cause to believe an untruth, or delude. What does God have to say about a life filled with deceit?

Romans 16:17-18 warns us of persons who would want to cause division among God's people. We are told to avoid this kind of person.

Paul writes in verse 17 that this person wants to "cause _____ and _____, contrary to the doctrine which you learned." In verse 18 Paul tells us that the deceptive person deceives to serve himself.

With what do they deceive? _____

What was David's prayer in Psalm 43:1?

_____

_____

_____

We need to pray that God will deliver us from those who would want to deceive you and me. Pray for discernment.

What does Jeremiah 17:9-10 tell us about deceit?

_____

_____

_____

Judas Iscariot deceived his fellow disciples for three years only to be found out when he betrayed the Son of God. When you choose to deceive, you are in direct conflict with God's character, which is truth. My friends, if you have made room in your heart to practice deception, repent and put on the belt of truth. Ask the Lord to forgive you. Be prepared for Satan's attacks. Anytime we repent and turn from sin, Satan will attack more aggressively. He doesn't give up easily. Arm yourself with truth.

Psalm 25:5, "Lead me into your _____ and teach me."

Psalm 40:11b "Let your lovingkindness and Your _____ continually preserve me."

Psalm 51:6a, "Behold, You desire _____ in the inward parts…"

John 4:24, "God is Spirit, and those who worship Him must worship in spirit and _____."

John 8:32, "And you shall know the _____ and the _____ shall make you free."

Ephesians 4:25, "Therefore, putting away _____, let each one of you speak _____ with his neighbor."

3 John 1:4, "I have no greater joy than to hear that my children walk in _____."

Lift high the banner of truth. Put off deception and mirror the character of God.

Day Two: The Wayward Heart

Today's Bible Reading: Matthew 26:34-75
Today's Banner: Ephesians 2:4, "God is rich in mercy."

Heart Repair

The people of Israel were not the only ones prone to wander. From the beginning of time to the present day church age, people have wandered away from His presence. Praise the Lord for His enduring mercy and lovingkindness.

From Adam and Eve to David to the Prodigal Son to Peter, wandering is one of the struggles of mankind. Why are we prone to wander? Is it because we think we know better than the Creator of the universe who is the lover of our souls? Do we get impatient with God's timing in our lives? Is it a rebellious spirit? Whatever your reason is or has been for wandering I pray you have found your way back and experienced his mercy and forgiveness.

I have often asked myself why Peter wandered away in such a public fashion. In Matthew 26 the account of Peter's denial is given.

Write down your observations and thoughts about Matthew 26:34-75.

_____
_____
_____
_____
_____
_____

Curiosity drove Eve to wander from God's protection.
Lust was the driving force in David's choice to wander.
Fear motivated Jonah to wander from God's plan.
Greed influenced the Prodigal Son to wander from a loving father who provided everything.

There are many reasons to like Peter. He was emotionally charged and passionate about whatever he did. He did not do everything right the first time, so for most of us it is easy to identify with Peter.

What are some areas that you see yourself in Peter?

_____
_____
_____

The Victor's Cry

Let's take a look at Peter's extraordinary journey with Jesus Christ. We first meet Peter (Matthew 4) at the seashore, working to provide for his family. We find him at the bedside of his mother-in-law (Matthew 8) in awe as Jesus heals her. In Matthew 14 Peter is not in the boat. He is walking on water. His boldness comes forth in Mathew 16 proclaiming that Christ is the Son of the living God. Forgiveness is explained to Peter in Matthew 18. Denial and sorrow grips Peters heart in Matthew 26. Peter followed Christ out of obedience. He lived for Christ out of love. He spread the gospel with passion, and he died because of his unwavering devotion to the one true God.

It does not matter who you are. We all can be prone to wander. On that dark day in Peter's life as he reflected on the night by the fire when he denied Christ, he was at his lowest. We don't know where Peter was when Christ hung on the cross. As a matter of fact, we don't know where any of the disciples were on that day. The Scriptures only tell us of John's presence. Peter didn't just wander on that night, Peter walked away.

Has there been a time in your life when you walked away from what you knew to be true?

_____

_____

_____

Peter could write 1 Peter 1:3 because he had lived it. Write this verse.

_____

_____

_____

I like the way the NLT words part of this verse: "...for it is by His boundless mercy..." Peter had experienced Christ's boundless mercy. Many people identify Peter as the one who betrayed Christ. Peter may have betrayed for a moment, but he lived for Him for a lifetime. Don't let your moment of weakness define you; let your life speak of God's boundless mercy.

Peter wandered away in spirit that dark night, but was reconciled through the blood of Jesus Christ. In 1 Peter 1:13-15 Peter reminds us how to live:

(vs. 13), "Gird up the _____ of your mind, Be _____ , and rest your hope fully upon the _____ that is to be brought to you at the revelation of Jesus Christ.

(vs. 14) Be _____ children, not _____ to the former lusts

(vs. 15) Be _____ in all your conduct.

Peter talks about the Lord's grace. In Chapter 2:1-3 Peter says to lay aside or put away malice, deceit, hypocrisy, envy, and evil speaking. Then Peter says, "If you have tasted that the Lord is gracious."

When have you tasted God's grace? _____

There is hope for the wayward heart. There is an open invitation to come home. I can only imagine the reunion that took place between Peter and his Lord after the resurrection. I'm sure there were tears of repentance, tears of rejoicing knowing he had been forgiven.

Peter wrote from his heart when he penned the words found in 2 Peter 3:9.

_____

_____

_____

You can experience Christ's longsuffering. His will is that all come to repentance. First, at salvation. Second, we can experience His forgiveness if we have ever chosen the path of the prodigal. The path of the prodigal has a U-turn option. Turn around, pick up the banner of grace and mercy, and run to your Savior's open arms.

Day Three: The Broken Heart

Today's Bible Reading: Isaiah 61:1-11
Today's Banner: Nehemiah 8:10, "Do not sorrow, for the joy of the Lord is your strength."

The good news of salvation according to Isaiah is that Christ came to heal the brokenhearted. Christ repeated Isaiah's prophecy in Luke 4:18. Compare Isaiah 61:1-2a to Luke 4:18-19. Are there any differences? Christ is the only true healer of the heart.

You may be experiencing a time in your life when your heart is breaking. Maybe it is a situation within your marriage, your children, your extended family, your church family, or a consequence due to sin. Whatever the reason for your heavy heart, there is a hope and One who can bring healing.

The Victor's Cry

Write Psalm 147:3.

_____

_____

_____

You serve Jehovah-rapha, the God who heals you.

What can we draw from the well of one's broken heart?

    Bitterness   Humility
    Anger   Repentance
    Resentment   Comfort
    Blame   Teachable spirit
    Misery   Joy

Whatever your water source is will determine what you draw out of the well. If your water source is bitterness, anger, resentment, blame, and misery then you will be adding more pain to an already painful situation. God is very clear on what these things will do to your heart.

Acts 8:23, "I see that you are _____ by bitterness."

Write the warning we're given in Hebrews 12:15.

_____

_____

_____

Bitterness is a root that can go deep within our lives, stealing our joy and bringing trouble to relationships. Bitterness is an internal disease that manifests itself outwardly and infects those around us.

Thumos, which is translated *to wrath,* is an outburst of wrath from inward indignation. *Thumos* may have the desire for revenge, though it may not act on those feelings. It quickly blazes up and quickly subsides.

Heart Repair

Proverbs 27:4a, "Wrath is _____ and _____ a torrent."

Eph. 4:26, "Be angry and sin not: do not let the sun go down on your _____."

James 1:20, "For the _____ of man does not produce the righteousness of God."

It is one thing to have a broken heart, but it is altogether different when you add your bitterness, anger, misery, and blame to that hurt. Don't pour alcohol on an open wound.

Ephesians 4:31 tells us to let all _____, _____, _____, clamor (quarrelling) and evil speaking be put away from you with all malice.

I watched a family member go through a time in her life when her heart was totally broken. I'm sure there were days she could hardly find the strength to get out of bed. I also witnessed what happens when a broken heart is handled with humility, comfort, joy, repentance, and a teachable spirit. Yes, it is possible to love the Lord with all of your broken heart. Of course, He desires to heal our hearts and will in His time. The most negative circumstance can be the most positive learning experiences in our walk with Christ if we look to the healer and not at the pain.

As a child, when I would hurt myself and have to be taken care of medically I would be told by whoever was taking care of the injury (usually Mom or Dad), "Look at me, not your injury." So it is with your broken heart. Look to the One who can heal with humility:

Psalm 9:12b, "He does not forget the cry of the _____."

James 4:6b, "God resists the proud, but gives _____ to the humble."

James 4:10, "_____ yourselves in the sight of the Lord, and He will lift you up."

In times of sorrow we need one another. I am so thankful for the friends the Lord has placed in my life to help bring healing to my broken heart.

What are we told to do in 1 Thessalonians 5:11?

_____
_____
_____

There are times our broken heart is a direct consequence of sin in our lives. For this reason repentance is the best medicine.

Psalm 34:18, "The Lord is near to those who have a _____, and saves such as have a _____ spirit."
Psalm 51:17, "The sacrifices of God are a _____, a broken and _____ heart–these, O God, You will not despise."

Sometimes the purpose of our broken heart is to teach us. Are you teachable? The Lord desires to teach us His ways and sometimes when we are in a place of hurt, He has our undivided attention.

Are you brokenhearted? What is God teaching you?

_____

_____

_____

Psalm 25:4, "Show me your _____, O Lord; _____ me your paths."

Even in the midst of your broken heart you can experience joy. That joy may come in the least expected places through the most unexpected people. But God does promise that joy does come and will be experienced.
Psalm 30:5 tells us that anger is for a moment; His favor is for life, weeping endures for a night, but joy comes in the morning.
Isaiah 61:3 comforts us to know that Jesus came to console those who mourn, to give beauty for ashes, oil of joy for mourning, and a garment of praise for the spirit of heaviness
James 1:2 says to count it all joy when you are tested. Are you finding joy in the God of your salvation?
Lift up your head and let the Lord anoint you with joy, give you beauty for your ashes, and dress you in a garment of praise. Commit to walk in the path of the brokenhearted with humility and a teachable spirit. Fight Satan's temptations of bitterness, anger, resentment, and blame. Raise your banner high.

Day Four: The Resting Heart

Today's Bible Reading: Psalm 55:1-23
Today's Banner: Psalm 55:22a, "Cast your burden on the Lord."

Jesus said, "Come to Me, all you who labor and are heavy laden, and I will give you rest." (Matt. 11:28). The Son of God acknowledges that we will get weary. Things will come into our lives that will weigh us down. Aren't you glad that Jesus is not bothered by our weariness or our burdens? His desire is for us to come to Him.

What is your burden? Why are you weary?

_____
_____
_____

There are many things that I understand more clearly (about God) now that I have had children. I still do not completely comprehend the depth of His love. Instead of trying to understand His love, I am overwhelmed by His love. We as parents know how much we love our children. Yet, God loves us even more.

When our daughter was younger, I knew she needed help carrying her toys. Her arms would be full, for she would have piled the toys so high she could not see where she was going. I would ask her if I could help and she would say, "No, I can do it myself." Meighan would get frustrated after she had dropped something for the third or fourth time and then she would let me help her. As moms do, I would take everything out of her tiny arms and take it to where she wanted it.

Are you carrying something that is too big, too heavy? Is your Heavenly Father saying to you, "Let me help you with that burden." With stubbornness are you telling the Lord, "No, I can do it myself." Yet all the while you're getting more and more frustrated, feeling as if no one cares or takes notice that you are weighed down.

What is your burden? Why haven't you given it to the Lord?

_____
_____
_____

Has there been a time when you did give your burden to God? What difference did it make?

_____

_____

_____

I like the fact that Christ says He will give rest. Does this mean that when you come to God with your burden of family situations, work related situation, or personal burdens that you won't have to deal with that burden again? As long as you live on this earth there will be burdens. When you carry your burden alone, the end result will be weariness. Rest from your burden is found when you come to Jesus with your burden.

How do you find rest in the Lord?

_____

_____

_____

I once heard someone say that we can lay our burdens down at the feet of Jesus all the time, but we often pick our burdens up and walk away with them. The Lord wants to take our burdens for us. When we give Him our burdens, does that mean we don't have emotions about it or think about it? Of course not, I do think that when you truly come to Christ and give Him whatever is weighing you down, there is rest and peace in your spirit. When there is true rest in the Lord, there is trust, security, and calm in the midst of life.

Can you think of a time in your life when you have experienced true rest?

_____

_____

_____

There are few guarantees in life, but this is one you can take to the bank. Christ says, "Come to me and I will give you rest." There are no stipulations to His promise. But the only way to have rest is to go to Him.

Give Him your burden and rest.

Day Five: The Restored Heart

Today's Bible Reading: Matthew 18:12-14; Luke 15: 11-32
Today's Banner: Psalm 51:12a, "Restore to me the joy of your salvation."

Webster's Dictionary gives the following definition of restore: to give back; to put back into use or service; to put or bring back into a former or original state. Do you need to be put back into use or service or brought back into your former or original state? When the Lord restores you that is exactly what He does. He will put you back into His service. In Psalm 51:12, the psalmist asks the Lord to restore the joy of His salvation.

Can you recall the joy you felt when you accepted Christ as your Savior?

It doesn't matter what you've done or where you have been, if you want to return to the ways of your Heavenly Father, He is waiting to restore you. The past weeks we have studied and seen God restore Jonah. He wasn't just put back into service, he was thrown back. The widow's faith was restored when Elijah asked for a meal, and David was restored after choosing to live in sin. You can never go too far to be out of His reach.

This is the story of a young man who was restless, running, rescued, and restored. The Prodigal Son is probably the parable of all parables. If you grew up in church this was probably one of the first Bible stories you learned. Let's look at this story again.

What does Luke 15:11-12 tell us about the young man?

For some reason, home wasn't where his heart was anymore. He was restless, and he knew there was money in the bank with his name on it. Jesus doesn't tell us what made the son want to leave home. There are different reasons that any one of us could become restless in our Christian life and want to walk away.

Have you been restless and walked away? What was your reason then or now?

_____

_____

_____

What amazes me about the beginning of this story is the Father's willingness to give his son what he wanted. That father did not control his son, just as our Heavenly Father chooses not to control you or me. God created you with your own free will. You have the choice to love the Lord with all your heart, soul, mind, and strength. The son asked for his money, and he was given what he asked for. I have wondered if the father stayed up late into the night thinking about what to do, but whatever his reasoning, the father granted the boy's request.

According to Luke 15:13, it did not take long for the son to pack his belongings and leave home. It amazes me that it never takes anyone long to leave, but it can take forever for them to come back.

Where did the son go and what happened in verse 13?

_____

_____

_____

He wasted all the money that his father had given him. When you choose to leave the safety and provision of your Heavenly Father, all that He supplies you with is wasted.

In verse 14, the young man had spent it all, and there was a famine. The NKJV states the latter part of this verse: "He began to be in want." The NLT writes, "He began to starve," and the Message is worded, "He began to hurt." When you make the choice to walk away from the Father you will find yourself wanting, starving, and hurting.

The table prepared for us by our Heavenly Father will be satisfying, nurturing, and nourishing. When you wander into that foreign land (away from the Father) you may find a few meals, but they will not give you satisfaction or nourishment. The famine in your soul will be so great that all you will do is want.

This young man became so desperate that he "joined himself to a citizen."

Write John 15:15.

_____

_____

_____

You are not of this world, and if you are living a life that is honoring to God, then the world knows you are different. This son thought that if he could be like them, then he would be fed. The world does not care about you or me. This citizen hired him and sent the young man into the fields to feed the pigs. Maybe the man was a farmer. Whatever the case, he didn't care about the young man only what he could get out of the young man.

What does Luke 15:16 say about the son's desperation?

_____

_____

_____

My great-grandfather had hogs. As a little girl I did not like to go near the hog pen. The smell was repulsive, and their eating habits were disgusting. The fact that this prodigal even entertained the thought of eating what the pigs were eating proves his desperation. The world welcomed him; the world hired him, but the world would not feed him.

Finally! We see a glimmer of hope. He comes to his senses in verse 17.

Write what Christ said.

_____

_____

_____

He realized that even his father's hired servants never went hungry. He had become a slave to the world, and he was perishing with hunger. When you serve the King of kings there is more than enough to eat, but when you are a hired help for a hungry world, it is every man for himself.

Verse 18 says, "I will _____ and _____ to my _____ and will say to him, 'Father, I have sinned against Heaven and before you.'"

Your first step home is confession. This young man's contrite spirit is evident in his humility.

What is he planning to ask his father once he is home (vs.19)?

_____

When you truly repent and desperately desire to return to the Father, others will see humility evident in every area of your life. You will serve with humility; you will give with humility; you will love with humility, and you will worship from a humble heart. The son did not care about the status he had with his father. The son only wanted to be in the presence of his father. Servants did not have any status with their master, but they could at anytime be in his presence.

What did the father do in verse 20?

_____

_____

_____

When you choose or if you have had to choose to walk down that road back to your Father, He is waiting, watching for you, and ready to show you compassion. Your Heavenly Father has your robe prepared to cover your shame, sandals ready so you can walk with Him, and a ring is made to prove you belong to Him. He sees your starving soul and—as the father did for the son—your Father wants to nourish your weary soul. I'm sure there were some long conversations that followed in the days to come, but for that day, the father focused on his son's return rather than on his son's running.

What did the father say in verse 24?

_____

_____

_____

Heart Repair

The following verses (25-32) focus on the brother's response to the prodigal's return home.

What was the response? (vs. 28)

_____
_____
_____

If you have never been the prodigal, maybe you know a prodigal. What is your response when a brother or sister in Christ returns to the Father?

_____
_____
_____

Are you angry? Are you jealous? (vs. 29) Are you happy? Are you excited to see what God is going to do in their lives?

Write your testimony below and if necessary thank your Heavenly Father for welcoming you back home and restoring you back to His service, or thank Him for keeping you close to Him at all times.

_____
_____
_____
_____
_____

WEEK SIX

All of My Soul

Day One: Just As I Am

Today's Bible Reading: Ruth 3:1-18, 4:1-12
Today's Banner: Ruth 3:10a, "Blessed are you of the Lord, my daughter!"

God desires your heart, soul, mind, and strength just as it is. With his overwhelming love He wants to shape our mind, heart, soul, and strength to be just as He planned it. Present yourself just as you are to the Creator and lover of your soul and watch in amazement as the Potter shapes something beautiful for His delight.

All we can do is come to the Lord just as we are. There is absolutely nothing that you and I can do to cause God to love us more, give us more, bless us more, or forgive us more. We are totally dependent on Him.

I have found great solace in the great hymns of the faith. I enjoy praise and worship songs, but I love the theology that can be found in hymns. The writers of the hymns most often wrote the lyrics out of the tragic times or the questionable times in their lives.

As written on Tanbible.com in Amazing Hymn Stories, Charlotte Elliott's brother, Rev. Elliott, was planning the building of a school for daughters of clergymen. The author was then forty-five years old, ill of health, and could not help. A special program had been scheduled to help in the fund-raising. That night she could not sleep and started doubting if she would be useful to the Lord. The next day, everyone went to the program, and she was alone. As she thought of her weakness, she realized that since salvation was not of works, her Christian life was also to be by faith and trust, that God accepts the weakest person.

Taking up her pen, she wrote this hymn of commitment. "Just as I Am" was published without Charlotte's name and was handed to her one day in leaflet form by her doctor, who did not realize that she was its author. Tears streamed down her face as she read the six verses and was told that copies of this poem were being sold and the money given to St. Mary's Hall. Miss Elliott then realized that she had at last made a significant contribution to the building of the school through the medium of her words of faith and humility.

> Just as I am, without one plea,
> But that thy blood was shed for me,
> And that Thou bidd'st me come to Thee,
> O Lamb of God, I come, I come!

Is there anything keeping you from coming to God just as you are?

_____

_____

_____

> Just as I am, and waiting not,
> To rid my soul of one dark blot,
> To Thee whose blood can cleanse each spot,
> O Lamb of God, I come, I come!

Is there anything you need to take to the Lord for cleansing?

_____

_____

_____

> Just as I am, tho' tossed about,
> With many a conflict, many a doubt,
> Fightings within and fears without
> O Lamb of God, I come, I come!

All of My Soul

What conflicts and doubts do you have that you need to take to the Lord?

_____

_____

_____

> Just as I am, poor, wretched, blind,
> Sight, riches, healing of the mind,
> Yea, all I need in Thee to find,
> O Lamb of God, I come, I come!

What do you need to find in the Lord today?

_____

_____

_____

> Just as I am, Thou wilt receive,
> Wilt welcome, pardon, cleanse, relieve,
> Because thy promise I believe,
> O Lamb of God, I come, I come!

What promise has God given you and what has been your journey to belief?

_____

_____

_____

> Just as I am, Thy love unknown,
> Hath broken every barrier down;
> Now to be Thine, yea, Thine alone,
> O Lamb of God, I come, I come!

What barriers has His love broken down? Are there any barriers that you need to let His love break?

_____

_____

_____

Day Two: The Potter's House

Today's Bible Reading: Jeremiah 18:6
Today's Banner: Philippians 1:6, "He who has begun a good work in you will complete it."

Jeremiah 18:6 is a question that tests our will. Read the verse and fill in the blank with your name.

"O _____, cannot I do with you as this potter? Saith the Lord. Behold, as the clay is in the potter's hand, so are ye in mine hand, O _____.

Are you willing to be the clay and allow God to mold and shape you as He wills? Do you really want to let God be in control?   Yes.   No.   Sometimes.   Not Sure.

Explain:

_____

_____

_____

Is there anything you need to give God the control of?

_____

_____

_____

Why is it difficult to be the clay?

_____

_____

_____

A potter has a unique craft. A potter completes four steps before he is finished with his creation. The first step is called centering. If the clay is not centered when the potter begins, then the clay will be off balance, and the potter will fight the clay the whole time. What a concept! You and I must be centered in the Lord Jesus Christ. When we are not centered in Him, everything in our life is off balance. Our attitude, our service, our priorities—everything is affected.

Are you off center? What in your life needs to be centered on the Lord Jesus Christ?

_____

_____

_____

It takes the potter's whole body to center the clay. While the wheel is spinning slowly, the potter pats the clay into a cone and forces it to the center of the wheel. It takes everything the potter has to begin the process of making something unique and beautiful. So it is with the God of the universe. Since the beginning of time, God has given His all to us and for us.

For me, the wheel is a symbolic representation of life. One thing I have come to realize as I get older is that life doesn't stop for anyone or anything. When a loved one dies, life still goes on. When a great tragedy in the world takes place—such as September 11 or hurricanes, devastating fires, or anything else—life still goes on. Life doesn't stop, has never stopped, nor will stop for anyone or anything.

The turning of the wheel is a key element in the outcome of the potter's craft. So it is with you and me. We have to strive to stay centered in the midst of life's business, chaos, routine, and interruptions. Life and all that goes with it pulls us in all directions, but the moment we begin to go too far to the right or left of that wheel we immediately are off center. God may use different things in our life to apply that pressure to cause us to return to Him–our center.

Draw a wheel. Write your name in the center of the wheel. Around the wheel write all of the things that are trying to pull you off center.

Aren't you glad that the Potter has both hands on the clay at all times? There may be a few of you due to your natural submission to the Lord that only need one hand, but for the majority we need both of His hands to keep us centered. Once the potter has the clay centered, he will want to open the clay. His hands must be totally still. The hole he is creating will wobble around, even though the outside of the clay appears to still be centered. The true test of the clay's center comes when the potters looks on the inside. Are you or have you ever only appeared to be centered? Others may look at you and think "Wow her life is spinning all around her, and she has it all under control" when you know in reality you are spinning out of control.

Are you only appearing to be centered?

_____

_____

_____

This step in pottery can be very tricky. I am so thankful that the Master Potter is no amateur. For the clay to be useful it has to be opened. Once again it takes both hands and pressure to accomplish this task. I find it interesting that we desire for God's hand to be on our life but we don't want Him to apply pressure to our life.

When the potter sits down at the wheel with a clump of clay in his hand only he knows what he desires to create. Pressure must be applied to make the clay open and useful. God desires for us to not only be moldable but to be open to Him and useful for the kingdom of God.

Is God applying pressure in your life to make you more open to Him and more useful to others? If so, what is He doing?

_____

_____

_____

If centering and opening was done well, pulling up the walls will not be too difficult. I chuckle at that. If we are centered and we are open, then the pulling is not difficult. I have yet to meet anyone who has no difficulty when they are being pulled or stretched. Yet, according to the world of pottery, this should be and can be one of the easiest processes. As people, we tend to create trouble for ourselves in this area. Maybe our prayers go something like this: *Lord, keep me centered on You. Mold me and open me to serve you and others, but, Lord, please don't stretch me. Don't pull me.* That kind of prayer and attitude are opposite to the desire Jabez had.

Read 1 Chronicles 4:10. What did Jabez ask God to enlarge?

_____

_____

_____

Was Jabez asking God to pull him, stretch him?   Yes.   No.

How is God pulling you?

_____

_____

_____

A potter will repeat the pulling until he reaches the desired thickness. I believe God does the same with you and me. He repeatedly pulls us until we meet His desire for us. Paul tells us in Ephesians 2:10 that we are his workmanship.

Write Ephesians 2:10.

_____

_____

_____

Pressure is applied differently depending on the way the clay will be used. By applying pressure to the outside, the opening of the piece becomes narrow. Applying pressure to the inside and gently pressing out will widen the piece. God can and does use outside and inward pressure to create us for His desired purpose.

Is your pressure coming from the outside or inside? What is your pressure? How can it be used for God's glory?

_____

_____

_____

The last step in the pottery process is called trimming. Trimming is done when the clay is leather hard. Trimming finishes the shape of the piece. I wouldn't think any of us are ready for trimming. None of us are finished. We are all a work in progress. I have a tendency to think that trimming takes place when we are called home. Only then will we be a finished work.

What does Philippians 1:6 promise us?

_____

_____

_____

I love the children's song:

> "He's still working on me
> To make me what He wants to be.
> It took Him just a week
> To make the moon and the stars
> The sun and the earth
> And Jupiter and Mars.
> How loving and patient He must be,
> He's still working on me."

Day Three: A New Creation

Today's Bible Reading: 2 Corinthians 5:17
Today's Banner: Revelation 21:5, "Behold, I make all things new."

All of My Soul

God created something from nothing. God spoke the world into existence. He breathed life into Adam and made Eve from Adam's rib. As incredible as all that sounds—and for some it may be unbelievable—the same God who created the universe and every living thing is most interested in the new creation of me and you. David asks the Lord to create in him a new heart.

Paul writes the promise in 2 Corinthians 5:17, "Therefore, if anyone is in Christ, he is a new _____; old things have passed away; behold, all things have become new.

I find it humbling that He is more interested in you and me than in anything else. We are the apple of his eye!

His creation of the world is beautiful. The miracles God performed in the Bible leave us speechless. We stand in awe of His power. But, Dear Friend, the greatest miracle and best creation looks back at you when you stand before the mirror. You, My Dear Friend, are his finest moment.

The moment you received Jesus Christ as your Savior you became a new creation. You are spectacular in His eyes. Your purity is breathtaking. The beauty of your soul is His greatest achievement. You are His creation!

Are you a new creation? When is your time of creation?

_____

_____

_____

I never want to take for granted that everyone who sits in a church pew or in a Bible study is a new creation in Christ. Dear friend, if you have not accepted God's free gift of salvation, please do so. Romans 3:23 tell us that all have sinned. Sin separates us from God. Romans 6:23 explains that the wages of sin is death, but the gift of God is eternal life through Jesus Christ. In Romans 10:9-13 we are shown how to accept God's gift. Confess with your mouth the Lord Jesus. Believe in your heart that God raised Jesus from the dead. If you have asked the Lord to forgive you of your sins and come into your life as Lord and Savior, then tell someone. Romans 10:11 says that whosoever believes on Him will not be ashamed. You are a new creation. Show the world your beauty!

I think it would be terrible if no one were allowed to enjoy the beauty of the Grand Canyon, the splendor of the mountains, and the incredible beauty of the ocean. My husband and I love the outdoors. I love to fall asleep to the sound of the ocean waves whenever we go to the beach. And there is nothing more beautiful than mountains. When we lived in Pennsylvania, I never got tired of the mountains. Their beauty was overwhelming. My favorite time of year in Pennsylvania is fall. I had never seen such indescribable colors. The colors were bold and bright. Growing up in Georgia, I never knew that leaves could look so extraordinary. We had a tree in our front yard that would turn the brightest orange I had ever seen. I would love to sit in the swing on our front porch and admire the color.

Is that God's purpose for you as His creation? Does He want to show you off? Is there something He has created in you (your spiritual gift, a talent) to be seen outwardly, for others to admire? What is your spiritual gift? What talents do you have to serve the Lord with?

_____

_____

_____

_____

When God creates in us a new heart, all things become new.

What does it mean for "all things to become new"?

_____

_____

_____

No, you don't get a new body, hair style, house, financial situation, or daily life. What you do get is a new way to look at life.

I hate the dark! There is a night light in just about every room in our house because I like to see what is in the room if I have to get up during the night. When you accepted Christ as your Savior, He didn't necessarily change what was in your life, His truth in your life revealed what needed to be changed in your life. When you walk into a dark room, you may know because of familiarity if there are chairs or tables or whatever else is there, but when you turn the light on you then see the reality of the condition of that furniture: dirty, clean, stable or unstable, old or new.

All of My Soul

Be the creation God made you to be and live in the light of His love and purpose for your life. Let the inward beauty of His creation in you work its way out so others are in awe of God's work in your life.

What is God's work in your life?

_____

_____

_____

Psalm 40:3, "He has put a _____ in my mouth–Praise to our God; many will _____ it and fear, And will _____ in the Lord."

Ephesians 4:23-24, "And be _____ in the spirit of your mind, and that you put on the _____ man which was _____ according to God, in true _____ and _____."

When you begin to let the inward beauty of God's new creation in you work its way out what will others see? (Read Colossians 3:12.)

_____	_____
_____	_____
_____	_____
_____	

Put on the characteristics of a new creation and let God show off His handiwork. When Satan comes to you and reminds you of your past and wants to cast doubt on the work God is doing in your life, carry your banner high.

Write a prayer of praise for all that God has made new in your life.

_____

_____

_____

_____

_____

Day Four: His Delight

Today's Bible Reading: 1 Samuel 15:1-23
Today's Banner: 1 John 1:7a, "Walk in the light as He is in the light."

The Lord has blessed my husband and me with two delightful children. I find them most delightful when I see growth in areas when they have a choice between right or wrong, and they choose to do the right thing. We can teach them all day long the difference between right and wrong, explaining the consequences of both, but the choice is completely theirs to decide when faced with a decision. I want to be God's delight.

What does the Lord delight in?

Psalm 37:23 _____

Psalm 147:11 _____

Proverbs 11:20 _____

Proverbs 12:22 _____

Proverbs 15:8 _____

Jeremiah 9:24 _____

He delights in truth. He delights in lovingkindness. He delights in righteousness. He delights in you when you walk in His way. He delights in you when you reflect all that He is teaching you.

In Numbers 14 Israel is not convinced by Joshua and Caleb that they can inherit the Promised Land. In Numbers 14:8, Caleb and Joshua were speaking to the children of Israel and the two men said,

"If the Lord _____ in us then He will bring us into this land and give it to us, a land which flows with milk and honey."

There is so much that your Heavenly Father longs to give you. Does the Lord delight in you?

Secondly, the Lord delights in our sacrifice, but He has greater delight in our obedience.

All of My Soul

What did the Lord tell Saul to do 1 Samuel 15:18?

_____

_____

_____

Did Saul obey the command?

_____

_____

_____

What did Saul and his men save?

_____

_____

_____

What did the Lord tell Samuel in 1 Samuel 15:11?

_____

_____

_____

What is better than sacrifice? (vs. 22)

_____

_____

What is rebellion? _____

What is stubbornness? _____

Let's not let rebellion and stubbornness take root in our lives. I don't want to be the Lord's regret. I desire to be His delight. Let your obedience be motivated with all the things that God delights in.

Not only strive to be His delight, but delight in all of His ways. Find pleasure in doing what the Lord asks of you. Many in God's Word found delight in obeying the Lord.

Who took delight in the ways of the Lord? (2 Chronicles 17:5-6) _____

Who delighted in God's goodness? (Nehemiah 9:24-25) _____

What happens when you delight in the ways of the Lord? (Psalm 37:4) _____

When you are anxious, what delights your soul? (Psalm 49:19) _____

Live your life in such a way that when the Lord thinks of you, He smiles with delight.

Day Five: Salt of the Earth

Today's Bible Reading: Matthew 5:1-13
Today's Banner: Psalm 40: 10b, "I have declared Your faithfulness and Your salvation."

After Christ spoke the Beatitudes, He said to those listening "Ye are the salt of the earth." He continues on to say that if salt loses its flavor then it is good for nothing. I do not want to be good for nothing.

In Christ's day, salt was one of the most important staples of any economy. It was viewed as a sign of prosperity. Salt was necessary for survival. Roman soldiers were often paid their wages in salt. Salt preserves and adds flavor to food. Salt was used for medicinal purposes, giving and sustaining life.

Salt would be taken from the Dead Sea or marsh areas, but often it was impure because it had mingled with earth's substances like gypsum. The salt became alkaline and would lose its salty character, savor, and effect because of contamination.

Obviously, by what Christ said in Matthew 5:13, salt can become tasteless. So can our lives. A life contaminated by the world's system, values, and belief systems can become tasteless. If we are not careful we can become too concerned with worldly matters, and they will take precedence over our spiritual well being. First John 2:15 tells us not to love the world nor the things in it.

All of My Soul

What are some things that could become a worldly priority?

_____
_____
_____

There are two areas in which we can become a tasteless Christian. We lose our saltiness when we no longer exhibit a Christ-like character.

Christ-like Character	Worldly Character
_____	_____
_____	_____
_____	_____

Write Matthew 6:24.

_____
_____
_____

We cannot serve God and this world at the same time. A choice has to be made. We will either be salt ready to be used for seasoning, or we will be tasteless, good for nothing.

Half-hearted discipleship can lead to a life of tasteless Christianity. God must have all of us for us to experience all of Him. Paul gives a clear picture of the believer who is fully devoted to Christ. "I have been crucified with Christ; it is no longer I who live, but Christ lives in me; and the life which I now live in the flesh I live by faith in the Son of God, who loved me and gave himself for me" (Gal. 2:20). There is no way someone half-heartedly devoted to Christ could claim that.

Is your life salty or tasteless? How is it salty? If it is tasteless what areas need to be seasoned with the salt of God's Word?

_____
_____
_____

Salt is a preservative. Those of us who know the Savior can preserve society and make it productive for God. We can give or have flavor and meaning in life through a relationship with Christ.

God has made us His key instrument to create a thirst for God among people in a lost society. Salt is a symbol of character, and of spiritual and moral fiber according to the standards of the Word of God. Salt creates thirst. Water is needed to sustain life. By their walk with God a believer helps create a thirst in the lives of those around them. This thirst can be satisfied by drinking of the waters of life received through faith in Christ. Who are you making thirsty?

_____

_____

_____

Is your speech seasoned with salt drawing others to the well of salvation (Colossians 4:6)? How will salt become salty again? We may lose our saltiness, but we can never lose our salvation. Paul admonishes us in Romans 12:2 that we are not to be conformed to this world. We must renew our mind, be transformed.

How do we deal with contamination?
1 John 1:9 _____

_____

He is faithful when we are unfaithful. He is just when we live unjustly. He makes us pure when we are unclean. If you have lost your saltiness, then return to His Word and be made pure and of good use. Live in such a way that you create a thirst in others and then lead them to the well that never runs dry.

WEEK SEVEN

All of My Strength

DAY ONE: CHOOSING TO REJOICE

Today's Bible Reading: James 1:1-18
Today's Banner: Philippians 4:4, "Rejoice in the Lord always."

Are we really supposed to rejoice in the Lord always? Life happens. Frankly in most situations rejoicing is not the first response on my list. Do I really need to rejoice during rush-hour traffic, the death of a loved one, the illness of a child, the discouraging news from a doctor, the bills, or the dysfunctional family? I'm sure you could add more to the list. In this world, there is so much more to be negative about than positive. If Paul lived today, would he have written those same words?

Rejoice means to give joy, to feel joy or great delight, to gladden. Rejoicing can be an act or an emotion. In times of great distress and trial we won't feel the emotion of rejoicing. No one would expect you to burst into laughter when given sad news of a loved one or a bad medical report from your doctor. In fact, if you did burst into laughter one might say you were in denial or didn't understand. There will be times when we won't feel like rejoicing, but I am thankful to say that we can know the One who gives the rejoicing.

In Exodus 18:9, Jethro rejoiced because_____

1 Samuel 2:1, Hannah rejoiced in _____

1 Chronicles 16:10, The heart rejoiced in _____

1 Chronicles 29:9, The People rejoiced because _____

In Psalm 5:11, we can rejoice because _____

Psalm 28:7 tells us that we can rejoice because the Lord is _____

In Luke 15:9, the woman rejoiced over _____

1 Corinthians 13:6 says we are to rejoice in _____

James 1:2-3 tells us to count it all joy when we go through trials. The New Living Translation has it written. "Dear brothers and sisters, whenever trouble comes your way, let it be an opportunity for joy. For when your faith is tested, your endurance has a chance to grow." Trials offer the "opportunity for joy." I think all of us would welcome any and every opportunity to be joyful. According to James, we should look at our trouble or trial as an opportunity to grow a joyful spirit, not obstacles to hinder our faith.

How can your trials and troubles be an obstacle or an opportunity to be joyful?

_____

_____

_____

I would think that all of us want to have a deeper, stronger faith in God. Isn't it interesting that the test or trial has to come first?

I love sports. I especially love to watch the Olympics. I find just about any Olympic sport interesting, but gymnastics, swimming, and track and field are my top three to watch. Before the Olympic team is chosen to represent our country in swimming and track and field each athlete has to go through a series of meets where they are timed (time trials). You have to qualify, which means you have to beat the clock. These athletes give up everything to practice hours a day to meet a certain time. Just think of the exhilaration they must feel when they go through the trials and meet the time needed to be considered for the Olympic team. Then to be placed on that team and (for some) it comes down to one race or one event to be awarded the gold, silver, or bronze medal. You not only are showing the world what you can accomplish but you are representing your country. They have passed the trial, the opportunity came, and the victory is theirs.

I believe it is much the same with believers in Christ. The only difference for the believer is we have already made the team. That was taken care of when we accepted Christ as Savior. Yet each day a trial can come our way, a trial to test our faith's endurance. Will we have an opportunity to rejoice or an obstacle for hindering growth?

Hebrews 11:17-19	Abraham's trial	Abraham's result
Judges 6:11-16; 7:19-21	Gideon's trial	Gideon's result
Daniel 6	Daniel's trial	Daniel's result

Don't you know that any trial after the lion's den was a cake walk for Daniel? Gideon probably never questioned God's ability to use ordinary people to do the extraordinary. As we have discussed throughout this study, Abraham had life experiences that changed generations' views of Jehovah-jirah.

When used as the springboard for a life of rejoicing, our trials can make the toughest situations bearable. We can let the ordinary moment become an extraordinary testimony for what God can do with everyday people. Our choosing to live a life of joy and taking each trial as an opportunity to grow our faith can change a generation.

What is your trial?

_____

_____

_____

What is your opportunity for joy?

_____

_____

_____

What is the obstacle to growing your faith?

_____

_____

_____

Whether you realize it or not, others watch you when you face a trial. Granted, some trials are personal and only you and God are aware of it, but there will be times when others know. They are watching. Just as the Olympian represents his country, we represent the body of Christ. Make your brothers and sisters proud to know you went through the test with grace.

The day that Meshach, Shadrach, and Abed-nego were put in the fiery furnace, they were not screaming, "This isn't fair!" or talking bad about King Nebuchadnezzar, or singing the blues. These young men may have prayed for their accusers, sung hymns, or encouraged one another to focus on the God they worshipped. Who knows what they did in the fire, but we know that they didn't get burned nor were they consumed by the fire. The king looked into that furnace and saw four men instead of just the three Israelites. (Daniel 3:25) Nebuchadnezzar recognized the three men and had no doubt who the fourth person was.

When you and I are thrown into a fiery trial, have assurance that God is already in the furnace. When others look at your life and watch you go through your trial, may they recognize the One who is walking with you.

When in a trial, do you live in such a way that others can recognize God in your life?

_____

_____

Lift high your banner in the face of the Enemy as he wants to take advantage of you while you walk through the fiery trial.

Day Two: Choosing to Believe

Today's Bible Reading: Matthew 9:18-26
Today's Banner: Hebrews 13:6, "The Lord is my helper; I will not fear..."

C. H. Spurgeon claimed that ninety-eight percent of the people he met—including the criminals he visited in England's prisons—told him that they believed the Bible to be true. But the vast majority had never made a personal, life-changing commitment to Jesus Christ. For them, *believe* was not an active verb. How sad but true. I wonder if that might be true today in our churches.

The days following September 11, Americans welcomed prayer in the public square. You could talk about God just about anywhere and to anyone and not many would be offended. Even public officials and politicians joined hand in hand, forgetting the separation of church and state, while standing on the steps of the United States capital building and sang, "God Bless America."

Have we truly changed as a nation? I am not trying to make a political statement, just an observation. If we as a nation can be brought to our knees for one brief moment in time only to quickly return to our selfish ways and ambition, can't we do that as individuals? Do we actively believe in the Lord Jesus Christ and the power of His blood, or do we agree with that on Sundays only to live mediocre lives and struggle in our walk with God?

The following story told by comedian Ken Davis explains the concept of belief very clearly:

> In college I was asked to prepare a lesson to teach my speech class. We were to be graded on our creativity and ability to drive home a point in a memorable way. The title of my talk was, "The Law of the Pendulum." I spent 20 minutes carefully teaching the physical principle that governs a swinging pendulum. The law of the pendulum is: A pendulum can never return to a point higher than the point from which it was released. Because of friction and gravity, when the pendulum returns, it will fall short of its original release point. Each time it swings it makes less and less of an arc, until finally it is at rest. This point of rest is called the state of equilibrium, where all forces acting on the pendulum are equal.
>
> I attached a 3-foot string to a child's toy top and secured it to the top of the blackboard with a thumbtack. I pulled the top to one side and made a mark on the blackboard where I let it go. Each time it swung back I made a new mark. It took less than a minute for the top to complete its swinging and come to rest. When I finished the demonstration, the markings on the blackboard proved my thesis.
>
> I then asked how many people in the room BELIEVED the law of the pendulum was true. All of my classmates raised their hands, so did the teacher. He started to walk to the front of the room thinking the class was over. In reality it had just begun. Hanging from the steel ceiling beams in the middle of the room was a large, crude but functional pendulum (250 pounds of metal weights tied to four strands of 500-pound test parachute cord.).
>
> I invited the instructor to climb up on a table and sit in a chair with the back of his head against a cement wall. Then I brought the 250 pounds of metal up to his nose. Holding the huge pendulum just a fraction of an inch from his face, I once again explained the law of the pendulum he had applauded only moments before, "If the law of the pendulum

is true, then when I release this mass of metal, it will swing across the room and return short of the release point. Your nose will be in no danger."

After that final restatement of this law, I looked him in the eye and asked, "Sir, do you believe this law is true?"

There was a long pause. Huge beads of sweat formed on his upper lip and then weakly he nodded and whispered, "Yes."

I released the pendulum. It made a swishing sound as it arced across the room. At the far end of its swing, it paused momentarily and started back. I never saw a man move so fast in my life. He literally dived from the table. Deftly stepping around the still-swinging pendulum, I asked the class, "Does he believe in the law of the pendulum?"

The students unanimously answered, "NO!"

I love that illustration. It is one thing to believe in the theory of the pendulum. It is something altogether different to believe in the action of the pendulum.

My pendulum moment came on December 9, 2003. It was my favorite time of the year, Christmas. On this particular night my mother had come by to visit with me and her wonderful grandchildren while my husband was at our church building the stage set for the Christmas cantata. The phone rang and on the other line was my dermatologist. I had gone to see him a week earlier about a spot on my leg. He said, "Joy, I have bad news. The place on your leg came back melanoma. You've got cancer."

I really couldn't tell you much about the rest of the night. I know at some point my mother left, and my husband came home. I don't know which was harder, hearing those words or telling them to my husband. The days that followed were filled with fear of the unknown, tears, anxiety, and *what ifs*. If you have ever been told those words by a doctor, you understand all of my emotions.

I grew up in church. I was taught God's Word at home and at a Christian school. I attended and graduated from a Bible college. I knew that God is our rock. He is my calm in the storm. He gives peace that passes all understanding. After all, "All things work together for good…," "God is love," and "He is my Jehovah-rapha—my healer." I sat in the classroom of the Christian life and stated that I believed, but on December 9 I was put in the chair with my head against the wall.

Through the whispers of a disease, God said, "Do you believe?" Suddenly, in a moment, my belief had to become an action. With the pendulum of cancer coming straight for me, did I truly believe that God is who God says He is and what He says is truth? You see, I had a choice. I could sit in the chair of that time in my life watching a heavy weight come straight at me believing that God has a plan, a hope, and a future for my life. I could either sit and be still and see God who He really is, or I could bolt. I could run and hide and never know in that darkest hour if God would come through.

Do you have a pendulum moment? Are you currently in a pendulum moment?

_____
_____
_____

Are you sitting still allowing God to show you His power of promises or are you running?

_____
_____
_____

Psalm 46:10a, "Be _____ and _____ that I am God."

C.S. Lewis said it so well in *A Grief Observed.* "You never know how much you really believe anything until its truth or falsehood becomes a matter of life and death. It is easy to say you believe a rope to be strong as long as you are merely using it to cord a box. But suppose you had to hang by that rope over a precipice. Wouldn't you then first discover how much you really trusted it?"

My mother loves the picture of the rope made of three strands. Two of the ropes represent our life but the third strand represents Christ. Dear friend, you can have all the rope you need to make it in life, but if you don't have the third strand woven carefully throughout the other strands, your rope won't hold you when life dangles you over the precipice. I don't want to sound like doomsday is around the corner. I say all of that to tell you that for every pendulum moment you face in your life, there is a pendulum promise.

Write Hebrews 13:5.

_____
_____
_____

Write a prayer naming all the reasons to believe God for who He says He is.

_____

_____

_____

_____

_____

_____

Day Three: Choosing to Obey

Today's Bible Reading: Deuteronomy 6:1-25, Romans 12:1-2
Today's Banner: 1 Samuel 15:22b, "Behold, to obey is better than sacrifice."

When God asks you to do something for Him, whether serve in an area of your church or something outside of church, do you question Him? Do you struggle with the choice to obey or not to obey? This can be one of the most difficult areas of the Christian life. For some, this is never an issue, but for others it is a struggle. There are times when God will simply say, "Do," or "Go," and wait to give the details until after we obey.

One of my favorite times of year at our church is the month of November. During November, we celebrate missionaries. Our church will host several missionary families. We roll out the red carpet. We honor the wives. We have Christmas for the families, and we honor a missionary of the year. As a church body, we give to meet their needs and love them.

I listen intently to their testimonies as they take us on the journey God has led them through. Most of the time, there is at least one couple who share that they struggled when God said, "Go." They asked the common question most of us would ask: "Where?" They wonder how it could financially be possible. Every story ends the same. God said, "Go." They obeyed. God gave direction and He provided every step of the way.

Many of us have not been chosen to go to a foreign land as some have been. We should all be willing to obey that call if God said, "Go." Do not forget, we have all been commanded to spread the gospel. Just because we live in the United States of America does not exempt us from the mission field. Our families, community, and country are a mission field.

First Corinthians 10:31 is a great reminder. "Whether therefore ye _____, or _____, or _____ ye do, do all to the glory of God."

It is for His glory! Ministry is to bring people to God to show them His glory.

When we are in a place where the only explanation is *God did this*, the joy that one finds is indescribable. The testimony is greater than ever imagined. God's glory and provision is seen by all.

As a teenager I learned one of my favorite songs. However, I never understood the true message until years later. It was written by St. Francis of Assisi:

> There's a voice calling me from an old rugged tree,
> And it whispers, "Draw closer to me."
> Leave this world far behind.
> There are new heights to climb
> And a new place in Me you will find.
> For whatever it takes to draw closer to you, Lord
> That's what I'll be willing to do.
> For whatever it takes for my will to break
> That's what I'll be willing to do.
> I'll trade sunshine for rain.
> I'll trade comfort for pain,
> Lord, that's what I'll be willing to do."

The words are powerful. Are we truly willing to allow the Lord to do whatever it takes to break our will? Do we really want to be broken, spilled out, and used up for Him? A choice has to be made: either allow God to break your will, setting you free from yourself, or go your own way and live an unsatisfied, superficial, entangled spiritual life. The journey is difficult. The temptation is to give up and go back to the comfort zone. Making the right choices, at times, can feel like spiritual boot camp that requires us to detoxify from the worldly influence that fills our life.

Write Romans 12:2.

_____

_____

_____

I have found that when I am reluctant to obey the Lord, it is a reflection of my walk with Him. I have realized that many times—more than I care to admit—my spiritual walk has been about me.

Have there been times when "you" kept getting in the way of what God wanted you to do?

_____

_____

_____

Believe it or not, there are times when it is easier to serve people than to love them. Anytime God calls us to a ministry, it is not only to serve Him by serving others; we are to love. I cannot count the times I have heard our pastor say, "Love God and love people." How true that is. There is another great quote that I have heard over the years. "People do not care how much you know until they know how much you care." The person who said that most likely had learned from experience.

Luke 10:27 tells us to love the Lord your God with all your heart and with all your soul and with all your strength and with all your mind and your neighbor as yourself. There is no coincidence that loving others is included alongside this commandment. God knew we would love ourselves. It is so difficult to love others as we love ourselves.

As a Christian we can look at a ministry and see all the benefits and the great things that it has to offer. Regardless of how exciting a ministry can be, if there is no love for the people and a heart to minister, then the ministry is dead. Everyone's situation can be different. Some people and situations can be easier to minister to than others.

I find it somewhat humorous that in Luke's writing of the commandment to love the Lord that "loving others as yourself" was added. God has known since the Fall of Man in the Garden that we are selfish. To love someone as you love yourself has got to be one of the most difficult things to do. Once again, we have to make a choice. The choice is to love or not to love.

Matthew 5:44, "_____ your enemies."

John 13:35, "By this all will know that you are My disciples, if you have _____ one for another."

Romans 13:8, "Owe no one anything except to _____ one another, for he who _____ another has fulfilled the law."

1 John 4:21, "And this commandment we have from Him: that he who _____ God must love his brother also."

1 Corinthians 13:13, "…The greatest of these is _____."

You can choose to obey God in all areas of your life—your heart, your soul, your mind and your strength—but if you obey and serve in every point and love is not the motivation, then it doesn't count. God doesn't want you to give your heart, soul, mind, and strength out of obligation. He wants you to give your all because you love Him and desire a relationship with Him.

Abraham chose to obey God's call to go because He loved the Lord. David chose to obey God's call to repentance because He desired a right relationship with God. Peter chose to follow Christ to the end of the earth because he was overwhelmed with love for his Master.

What is your reason for obedience?

_____
_____
_____

Do you love others through the ministry God has called you to?   Yes.   No.

Explain.

_____
_____
_____

Take this time to focus on your love for God. Do you love Him with all your heart, soul, mind, and strength? Does this love motivate to absolute obedience?

_____
_____
_____

Day Four: Choosing to Serve

Today's Bible Reading: Genesis 29
Today's Banner: Psalm 100:2a, "Serve the Lord with gladness."

Have you ever sung the chorus, "Make Me a Servant Humble and True"? It can be easier to sing those words than to put those words into action. That is what you and I are called to do: serve.

Genesis 29 is one of my favorite Bible stories because it challenges my servant attitude. Jacob was the son of Isaac and Rebecca, grandson of Abraham. Jacob was on a journey because he had deceived his father, Isaac, in order to receive the blessing that was meant for his older brother, Esau. Jacob was not on a leisure journey. He was running for his life. Esau was very angry with Jacob and said he would kill Jacob.

Who did Jacob see and who was she? (Genesis 29:9-10)

_____

_____

_____

Rachel immediately told her father that his nephew was there. Jacob was immediately welcomed into their home, and he stayed for one month. Laban asked Jacob what he should be paid for all the work he was doing there.

What was Jacob's response? (Genesis 29:18)

_____

_____

_____

Obviously this was pleasing to Rachel's father because he asked Jacob to stay with the family. His love for Rachel is evident in verse 20.

Write Genesis 29:20.

_____

_____

_____

Jacob's love for Rachel motivated him to serve Laban with gladness. Does your service to the Lord seem only as a few days because you are serving the Lord with gladness? When Jacob had fulfilled his seven-year contract with Laban, he asked for Rachel's hand in marriage.

What happened at the wedding? (vs. 25)

_____

_____

_____

The custom of the land in which Laban and his family lived, the oldest daughter was to marry first.

What was Jacob's response? (vs. 27, 30)

_____

_____

_____

All total, Jacob served fourteen years for the love of his life. If there was an award to be given, Jacob would receive "Servant of the Year."

What can we learn from this story? Jacob's service to Laban kept him in a stable environment. Remember, Jacob came upon Laban's household because he was running from his brother, Esau. I know from personal experience that there have been times that my service in a ministry has held me accountable. When you are serving the Lord in an active ministry, you will think twice before you give into temptation to leave the family of God.

The Victor's Cry

Can you recall a time when your service to God kept you?

_____

_____

_____

Secondly, Jacob teaches us that service should be done with a right attitude. His service to Rachel's father seemed only as a few days. Your attitude is a key element to the effectiveness of your service.

Second Corinthians 9:7 says, "So let each one _____ as he purposes in his heart, not _____ or of _____; for God loves a cheerful giver."

Jacob gave his time, his service, his talent, not once but twice, and it was done with a right attitude.

Are you serving the Lord with a right attitude?   Yes.   No.   Sometimes.

Explain.

_____

_____

_____

Harry Emerson Fosdick once told how as a child, his mother sent him to pick a quart of raspberries. Reluctantly he dragged himself to the berry patch. His afternoon was ruined for sure. Then a thought hit him. He would surprise his mother and pick two quarts of raspberries instead of one. Rather than drudgery his work now became a challenge. He enjoyed picking those raspberries so much that fifty years later that incident was still fresh in his mind. The job hadn't changed. His attitude had, though, and attitude is everything.

Last of all, we see in this story that the father honored Jacob's request. He and Rachel were married. Yes, he had to work another seven years, but Jacob had already proven himself. Your service to the Lord never goes unnoticed. Many people may not pat you on the back or tell you thank you very often, but the One you serve sees all that you do. Your hard work will be rewarded one day. You will hear, "Well done thou good and faithful servant." Keep an attitude of gladness as you serve the Lord and let love be your motivation to serve.

Write a thank-you note to someone you know who gives their time serving the Lord. Your encouraging words may be the pick-me-up they need to hear.

Day Five: The Victor's Cry

Today's Bible Reading: Revelation 19:11-16
Today's Banner: Revelation 19:16, "KING OF KINGS AND LORD OF LORDS."

One day the banner will be raised, and we can say the battle is over. Righteousness has won. Evil has been conquered, and death can hold no one! My prayer has been that you have come out of this study a conqueror. You have stepped on battlefields, lifted your banner, and followed your Commander to victory. You have been shown that there is a battle plan and when you follow it you can be victorious. You don't have to live a defeated Christian life. You can live an abundant life. This is the King that leads us to victory as told by the great preacher, Dr. S.M. Lockridge, taken from *Glorious Appearing*, Left Behind Series.

My King is...

The Bible says my King is a seven-way king. He's the King of the Jews; that's a racial king. He's the king of Israel, that's a national king. He's the king of righteousness. He's the king of the ages. He's the king of heaven. He's the king of glory. He's the king of kings. Besides being a seven-way king, He's the Lord of lords. That's my king. Well, I wonder, do you know Him?

David said, "the heavens declare the glory of God, and the firmament showeth His handiwork." My king is a sovereign king. No means of measure can define His limitless love. No far-seeing telescope can bring into visibility the coastline of His shoreless supply. No barrier can hinder Him from pouring out His blessings.

He's enduringly strong. He's entirely sincere. He's eternally steadfast. He's immortally graceful. He's infinitely powerful. He's impartially merciful. Do you know Him?

He's the greatest phenomenon that has ever crossed the horizon of this world. He's God's Son. He's the sinner's Savior. He's the centerpiece of civilization. He stands in the solitude of Himself. He's honest and He's unique. He's unparalleled. He's unprecedented.

He is the loftiest idea in literature. He's the highest personality in philosophy. He is the supreme problem in higher criticism. He's the fundamental doctrine of true theology. He's the core, the necessity for spiritual religion. He's the miracle of the ages. Yes, He is. He's the superlative of everything good that you choose to call Him. He's the only one qualified to be our all-sufficiency, I wonder if you know Him today.

He supplies strength for the weak. He's available for the tempted and tried. He sympathizes and He saves. He strengthens and sustains. He guards and He guides. He heals the sick. He cleanses the leper. He forgives the sinner. He discharges debtors. He delivers the captive. He defends the feeble. He blesses the young. He serves the unfortunate. He regards the aged. He rewards the diligent. And He beautifies the meek. I wonder if you know Him.

Well, this is my king. He's the key to knowledge. He's the wellspring of wisdom. He's the doorway of deliverance. He's the pathway of peace. He's the road-way of righteousness. He's the highway of holiness. He's the gateway of glory. Do you know Him?

Well, His office is manifold. His promise is sure. His life is matchless. His goodness is limitless. His mercy is everlasting. His love never changes. His word is enough. His grace is sufficient. His reign is righteous. His yoke is easy and His burden is light. I wish I could describe Him to you.

He's indescribable. He's incomprehensible. He's invincible. He's irresistible. Well, you can't get Him out of our mind. You can't get Him off your hand. You can't outlive Him and you can't live without Him. The Pharisees couldn't stand Him, but they found they couldn't stop Him. Pilate couldn't find any fault in Him. Herod couldn't kill Him. Death couldn't handle Him, and the grave couldn't hold Him. That's my King!

And Thine is the kingdom and the power and the glory forever and ever and ever and ever! How long is that? And ever and ever! And when you get through with all the forevers, then amen! Good God Almighty! Amen!"

I can never read that sermon too much or hear it too often. What a powerful description of the King we serve.

That is the King who will lead you into victory! He will give you the ability to love Him with all your mind, conquering doubt, worry, insecurity, and pride. Your weapons are mighty in God, pulling down strongholds. Your King will cast down every argument and every high thing that exalts itself against the knowledge of God. He can bring every thought into captivity to the obedience of Jesus Christ (2 Corinthians 10: 4-5).

The King of all kings will restore your heart so you can love Him as He desires. You can approach His throne with boldness and have confidence that every good and perfect gift comes from your Father above (James 1:17). He will conquer the Deceiver who has you in chains and His truth will make you free. He is waiting for you to come to Him and rest, so that He can carry your burden.

This eternal King wants all of your soul. He desires you just as you are. He has a plan for you, and this plan is found on the Potter's wheel. It is there that you will be made a new creation, His delight.

With all of your strength, raise your banner and give your King your all. All of your service, all of your belief, total obedience. Hold nothing back. Rejoice in Him, the King of glory.

LIFT HIGH YOUR BANNER. FIGHT THE GOOD FIGHT

To order additional copies of

Have your credit card ready and call:

1-877-421-READ (7323)

or please visit our web site at
www.pleasantword.com

Also available at:
www.amazon.com
and
www.barnesandnoble.com